CW01501782

Con

Austin Farrer

Austin Farrer

Oxford Warden, Scholar, Preacher

Edited by

MARKUS BOCKMUEHL AND

STEPHEN PLATTEN
with Nevsky Everett

scm press

© Editors and Contributors 2020

Published in 2020 by SCM Press
Editorial office
3rd Floor, Invicta House,
108–114 Golden Lane,
London EC1Y 0TG, UK
www.scmpress.co.uk

SCM Press is an imprint of Hymns Ancient & Modern Ltd
(a registered charity)

Hymns Ancient & Modern® is a registered trademark of
Hymns Ancient & Modern Ltd
13A Hellesdon Park Road, Norwich,
Norfolk NR6 5DR, UK

British Library Cataloguing in Publication data

A catalogue record for this book is available
from the British Library

9780334058595

Typeset by Manila Typesetting
Printed and bound by
CPI Group (UK) Ltd

Caroline Farrer

In memoriam

4 April 1939 – 10 February 2018

Contributors

Ian W. Archer is Associate Professor and Tutor in History at Keble College Oxford, and an Honorary Vice-President of the Royal Historical Society. He has published widely on the social and cultural history of early modern London, including most recently *The History of the Haberdashers' Company* (2017) and an edition of a Frenchman's description of Elizabethan London, *The Singularities of London, 1578* (ed. with Derek Keene, 2014). He co-authored a history of Keble College with Averil Cameron, *Keble Past and Present* (2008).

John Barton was Oriel and Laing Professor of the Interpretation of Holy Scripture at the University of Oxford, 1991–2014, and is now a Senior Research Fellow at Campion Hall, Oxford. His recent books include *Ethics in Ancient Israel* (2014) and *A History of the Bible: The Book and Its Faiths* (2019; US edition: *A History of the Bible: The Story of the World's Most Influential Book*, 2019).

Markus Bockmuehl is Dean Ireland's Professor of the Exegesis of Holy Scripture at the University of Oxford and a Professorial Fellow of Keble College. Among his authored books are *Seeing the Word: Refocusing New Testament Study* (2006), *Simon Peter in Scripture and Memory* (2012), and *Ancient Apocryphal Gospels* (2017).

Nevsky Everett has been the Chaplain of Keble College since 2016.

Mark Goodacre is Frances Hill Fox Professor of Religious Studies at Duke University. He has published widely on the New Testament and Christian origins, and his books include *Thomas and the Gospels* (2012) and *The Case Against Q* (2002).

Michael F. Lloyd is Principal of Wycliffe Hall, Oxford. His academic work is mainly on the Problem of Evil. He recently co-edited *Finding Ourselves after Darwin* (with Stanley P. Rosenberg, 2018), on the theological implications of evolutionary theory and modern genetics for our understanding of the Image of God, Original Sin and the Problem of Evil. He is the author of a popular-level systematic theology entitled *Café Theology* (3rd edn 2012). He has also written on the theology of G. F. Handel.

Sir Jonathan Phillips has been the Warden of Keble College since 2010.

Stephen Platten was formerly Bishop of Wakefield and is an Assistant Bishop in the Dioceses of London, Newcastle and Southwark. His publications include *Augustine's Legacy: Authority and Leadership in the Anglican Communion* (1997); *Rebuilding Jerusalem: The Church's Hold on Hearts and Minds* (2007); *Animating Liturgy: The Dynamics of Worship and the Human Community* (2017). He is at present co-editing a further collection of essays on Austin Farrer with Bishop Richard Harries.

Judith Wolfe is Professor of Philosophical Theology at the University of St Andrews. She writes widely on philosophical and systematic theology, as well as on theology and the arts, particularly C. S. Lewis. On the latter, she has co-edited *C. S. Lewis and the Church* (with Brendan Wolfe, 2011), *C. S. Lewis's Perelandra* (with Brendan Wolfe, 2013) and *C. S. Lewis and His Circle* (with Roger White and Brendan Wolfe, 2015), and acts as General Editor of the *Journal of Inklings Studies* (Edinburgh University Press).

Acknowledgements

The editors wish to thank the Warden and Fellows of Keble College for their support of this project, both the original conference in January 2019 and the production of this volume.

More particularly, we are grateful to the College for a Keble Small Research Grant awarded to Markus Bockmuehl for this purpose. This made it possible to invite and host external speakers, and for conference facilities and refreshments to be available free of charge (graciously supported by Keble's catering and maintenance staff). The same grant also enabled the appointment of a graduate research assistant to help with the conference implementation and associated publicity, administration and support tasks, as well as with significant editorial work in the preparation of this volume.

We wish to pay tribute to the invaluable advice and assistance received from the Chaplain of Keble College, Nevsky Everett, who supported our work throughout the planning, conference and editorial stages of the project. Jennifer Strawbridge, a former Chaplain of Keble (now Associate Professor in New Testament Studies and a Fellow of Mansfield College), also provided wise and energetic counsel in the planning stages for the 2019 conference.

Jacob Rodriguez served most efficiently as our graduate assistant, recruiting and overseeing a team of additional student helpers on the day, and ably supporting all stages of the editorial process for the book.

The editors and contributors are grateful to Faye McLeod, the Keble College Archives and Record Manager, for her help in locating relevant material.

Kay Norman ably assisted in the task of editing the sometimes difficult and poorly preserved typescripts of Austin Farrer's four unpublished lectures of 1966, formatting and typing successive drafts.

We are most grateful to an anonymous Keble alumnus for a donation to the College specifically to provide the necessary publisher's print subvention to make this volume possible. We also thank the College's Development Director Jenny Tudge, whose assistance was catalytic in facilitating this donation.

Last but by no means least, we would like to express our gratitude to Nick Newton, Austin Farrer's nephew, for the Executors' permission to publish Farrer's four American lectures here for the first time.

Foreword

SIR JONATHAN PHILLIPS

For any Warden of Keble to suggest that a particular predecessor is pre-eminent would be unwise. However, the assertion that Austin Farrer was one of the most academically distinguished holders of the office should not be challenged. The affidavits in support of the claim would cite Rowan Williams's observation that he was 'possibly the greatest Anglican mind of the twentieth century' and the description of him by Basil Mitchell, his slightly younger contemporary, as being, 'by common consent, one of the most remarkable men of his generation'.

He was born on 1 October 1904 as the second child and only son of Augustine and Evangeline Farrer. He came up to Oxford from St Paul's School as a Scholar of Balliol. His results in Greats and, subsequently, in Theology were outstanding. With the exception of a brief period serving a curacy in Dewsbury, he spent the whole of his career at Oxford, holding Fellowships and the Chaplaincies at St Edmund Hall and then Trinity before becoming Warden of Keble in 1960.

During his first year as an undergraduate at Balliol he took the particularly important decision to be baptised an Anglican, disillusioned by the splits among the Baptists and attracted by the liturgy of the Church of England. The published correspondence between parents and son about that momentous decision is both touching and illuminating. Austin was under no illusion about the pain that would be caused to his father, a man who trained Baptist ministers, if his son were to leave the denomination. There was much agonising on both sides, but what is especially striking is the young Austin's care and sensitivity in dealing with his parents.

Such sensitivity was a feature of his sermons, which are the way in which many who are not theologians or philosophers by profession have encountered Farrer's thinking. How fitted he was to be a counsellor is well-illustrated by a sermon entitled 'Responsibility for our Friends'. In it is revealed a person who had thought deeply about what we now call student welfare and mental health issues and who offers sensible, practical advice based on his own experience of the death of a college friend shortly after graduating.

This volume had its origins in a conference held in the College in January 2019 to mark the 50th anniversary of his death on 29 December 1968. Fittingly, and making a valuable contribution to the celebration, publication will take place during the year in which Keble is marking the 150th anniversary of its foundation in memory of another great Anglican figure.

The contents place some emphasis on Farrer's time at Keble, most notably with Ian Archer's appreciation of his contribution as Warden and the splendid tribute to his intellectual endeavour during that period in the form of four lectures first given in the USA which are being published here for the first time. The other contributors, while making elegant mention of the Keble dimension, range more widely from their various perspectives. All offer fascinating insights into the man and, again quoting Basil Mitchell, his qualities of 'originality, independence, imagination and intellectual force'. We should all be grateful to Professor Markus Bockmuehl for having the inspiration and energy to see the project through to completion.

Sir Jonathan Phillips
Warden of Keble College (2010–)

Introduction

MARKUS BOCKMUEHL AND
STEPHEN PLATTEN

Austin Farrer (1904–68) served as Warden of Keble College from 1960 until his sudden death of a heart condition on 29 December 1968. The present volume celebrates his legacy in relation both to the 50th anniversary of his death in late 2018 and to the 150th anniversary of Keble College in 2020.[1]

Farrer's appointment to the Wardenship came at the culmination of a long and distinguished Oxford career that had successively seen him linked with Balliol College as an undergraduate, Cuddesdon as an ordinand, St Edmund Hall as a Chaplain and Tutor (1931–5), and Trinity College as a Fellow and Chaplain (1935–60).

Aside from his institutional service to Keble and other colleges, Farrer was a distinguished and well-known scholar of several different disciplines. He made lasting contributions to philosophy, Christian theology and Biblical Studies.

In New Testament circles, Farrer is best remembered for challenging the prevailing theory of a lost sayings source ('Q') behind the Gospels and for articulating a very brief but elegant alternative account for the literary origins of the Synoptics.[2] His exegetical interest was particularly attracted by the Gospel of Mark.[3]

Farrer's contributions to Philosophical Theology revolved around the topics of providence, free will, the Problem of Evil, and his theory of 'dual causation' or 'double agency' to understand divine action in the world.[4]

Interested as he was in the role of inspiration and imagination for literary artistry, he became a key associate and conversation partner in Oxford literary circles during and after the Second World War, as well as a close friend of C. S. Lewis. He is also remembered as a remarkable preacher throughout his long Oxford career – up until his last sermon at St Andrew's Headington a week before his death, which was broadcast on the BBC and presciently entitled 'The Ultimate Hope'.[5]

Not unlike many other polymaths then and now, Farrer found that his sometimes idiosyncratic originality tended to be viewed by specialist colleagues in the various disciplines with something between suspicion and disdain, as we will also see later in this volume. Nevertheless, with the benefit of half a century's hindsight his eclectic yet catalytic contributions to each of these fields turn out to have left an enduring mark on subsequent scholarship. (Stories like his might commend a sentiment of caution to Her Majesty's latter-day academic bottle-top counters, committed as they are to Research Excellence measurements involving instantaneous judgements of 'impact'.)

To mark the 50th anniversary of his death on 29 December 1968, an international day conference was held at Keble College on 18 January 2019. While this initiative arose from a recurrent short feature of Oxford's New Testament Seminar to commemorate influential biblical scholars, the idea of a conference soon took hold and plans grew in scope and size: around 90 registered conference participants heard speakers from Oxford, St Andrews and Duke University in the USA. Following a welcome by the Warden Sir Jonathan Phillips and an introduction by Ian Archer to Farrer's work as Warden of Keble, four other speakers each highlighted one of the major facets of Farrer's legacy in the Academy and the Church: his scholarship on the Gospels (Mark Goodacre); his role as an Oxford literary figure (Judith Wolfe); his work on the Problem of Evil (Michael Lloyd); and his profile as a preacher (John Barton). After the formal proceedings, the conference ended appropriately in Keble College Chapel with choral Evensong, including a sermon preached by Bishop Stephen Platten, one of the editors of the current volume.

Giants of an earlier age tend to make one feel that the life of the present is impoverished, and that 'we shall not see their like again'. In Austin Farrer's case, that question of legacy presses upon us with a peculiar urgency. Parts One and Two of this book amply illustrate Farrer as exceptional in combining his memorably incisive preaching in the University with lasting contributions to the study of the New Testament, philosophical theology and theology and literature. But would he be able to do so today? Does the Church of England still care to educate clergy of such scriptural and theological acuity? Conversely, do university departments of theology and religion any longer retain the ability to recognise and value their subject's reciprocal relationship to the core historic convictions held by living communities of faith?

In a recent volume on the challenge of holding together academic and pastoral vocation in the Church and Academy, one Oxford chaplain raises the pointed question, 'Where have all the Austin Farrers gone?' (Henson, 2016, 25). He goes on to highlight the contrast between Farrer and the present-day scholar-priests being steadily driven to extinction by a deliberate deprivation of 'habitat'. Pincer-like, that deprivation closes around them in the form of relentlessly detheologising departments of religion and, on the other hand, the process-focused managerial regimes of training for ministry.

A sense of panic in response to the secular has rapidly debased the Church's idea of 'mission' amid widespread gasping for the supposedly clean air of management and leadership. That 'mission' has in the Church of England narrowed to the point where 'relevance' becomes the primary criterion for the selection of its spiritual leaders: bishops, deans, residentiary canons. Theology, by contrast – the skilful, patient and public articulation of the love of God with the mind – seems non-essential and even counterproductive to that new currency of 'mission'. And thus Farrer's participation in the dialogue of faith and reason, church and university, comes to be actively devalued and disincentivised.

Fifty years after his death, Austin Farrer's profile contrasts sharply against the present century's accelerating re-estrangement of the Church from biblical scholarship, from the interdisciplinary engagement of philosophy or of literature – and conversely of serious intellectual engagement from the task of expounding the gospel in the Church. To those with eyes to see why these things matter, Farrer's work and example sound a call for change that could not be more timely.

We are delighted to be able to include in this volume not only the 2019 conference proceedings celebrating Farrer's work (Part One), but in addition a newly edited set of four lectures that Farrer delivered in the USA in 1966, and which are here published for the first time (Part Two).

Part One: Farrer at Keble – The Gospels, C. S. Lewis and Philosophical Theology

Ian Archer's opening chapter offers a vividly fascinating and bracing account of Farrer's eight short years as Warden of Keble, beginning with his narrowly successful election to that office against the background of a good measure of scepticism among the Fellowship. In the face of some continued opposition, and somewhat against the expectation of those who doubted his ability to focus on the task of administrative and institutional leadership, Farrer made a success of the job. Although admittedly intense, shy and impatient with the politics of college governance alongside certain eccentrically obstructive members of the Fellowship, he could nevertheless be remarkably hands-on and generous – for example, in his pastoral engagement, the hospitality he and Mrs Farrer extended to members of the College and University in the Warden's Lodgings, and his commitment even as a reluctant convert to the need for development and fundraising. Less surprisingly, perhaps, he was actively engaged in the Chapel, not least as a regular preacher. Above all, Archer stresses the distinctive commitment of key initiatives, relationships and practical wisdom that Farrer deployed as Warden in service of the Keble community.

Turning to the first of three chapters on Farrer's scholarship, Mark Goodacre begins with an examination of Farrer's contribution to New Testament studies through the often sceptical eyes of his contemporary critics. Doubtful about atomising dimensions of the mid-twentieth-century preoccupation with form-criticism, Farrer preferred instead to attend to macro-structural patterns and symbolism in the Gospel of Mark – even if not always persuasively. More influentially, Farrer explained the relationship between the Gospels of Mark, Matthew and Luke without reference to the classic nineteenth-century German hypothesis of Matthew and Luke both having used Mark along with a sayings source 'Q'. Instead, Farrer boldly proposed that it is simpler and more persuasive to see Luke as using Matthew, while both of them used Mark. Where once Synoptic Gospel criticism dismissed this theory out of hand, it has in recent years gained a substantial following in the wake of its reception and influential development by others (including, most influentially, Michael Goulder and indeed Mark Goodacre himself).[6] Goodacre underscores Farrer's work on the Gospels by reference to an unpublished manuscript on Mark. Despite its old-fashioned tone and underdeveloped ideas in many respects, Farrer's attention to the symbols and patterns of the evangelists' work was vital not only to his understanding of inspiration but would turn out to energise a new generation of scholarship on the Gospels.

Michael Lloyd explores Farrer's work on the Problem of Evil as one among several influential contributions to the field of philosophical theology. Farrer downplayed the idea that sin – original or otherwise – is to blame for human frailty and mortality: to him, it can only be seen as the cause of moral evil, but not of natural evil. Evil for him is not instrumental to God's purposes, but it is rather inevitable and even necessary for the vitality of the physical world that God in fact has created. Lloyd suggests that Farrer's steadfast refusal to instrumentalise evil within God's purposes represents one of the many strengths of his theodicy, as is the consoling importance of an eschatological resolution. Lloyd objects, on the other hand, that a Trinitarian conception of God more readily and more satisfactorily allows for an account of physical creation that prioritises peace over conflict and a less 'Platonised' eschatology.

Judith Wolfe documents the relatively little-known friendship between Austin Farrer and C. S. Lewis, including the former's pastoral care for Lewis both at his marriage to Joy Davidman, and at her death as well as at his. Lewis celebrated several of Farrer's writings and admired them for their theology as much as for their style.[7] Conversely, Farrer in turn appears to have been somewhat more critical of various aspects of Lewis's work – whom he regarded as a much better apologist than a theologian. And yet, Judith Wolfe persuasively drives home the point that the mutual engagement of Lewis and Farrer shows them both fundamentally concerned with an imaginative 'vision of the world' – whether in apologetics, in philosophy or in theology, and despite their significant disagreements on the role of what Farrer regarded as Lewis's 'superfluous unrealities' and myths that have 'become fact'. Farrer, she concludes, may in the end offer an important 'ascetic' correction to Lewis's extravagant theological imagination.

John Barton personally knew Farrer and in 1967 was tutored by him on the New Testament – before eventually embarking on a distinguished career as an Old Testament scholar. For the 2019 conference and this volume, Barton offers an appreciation of Farrer's extensive oeuvre of sermons. Despite his acoustically unimpressive presence in the pulpit, Farrer was a celebrated preacher. Several volumes of his sermons were published. Among these, Barton singles out a Christmas Day sermon entitled 'A Grasp of the Hand' to illustrate the power of this preacher's pastoral, rhetorical and imaginative engagement with his subject matter, showing that 'God does not work in the world or in us by massive frontal assault, but by making our wills in line with his – "by weakness not by strength"'. Without visible intervention or special revelations, God's action in the world is above all through the Christian life and its care for others. The themes of his philosophy, theology and New Testament scholarship showed themselves to be remarkably integrated in his preaching.

Part Two: Farrer in America – Four Unpublished Lectures (1966)

It is, to some degree, this integration of philosophical, doctrinal, biblical and ascetic theology that has assured Farrer of a perennial and seminal reputation and influence within the Academy. Rowan Williams devotes to him much of the opening chapter of his 2018 monograph *Christ the Heart of Creation*; indeed he ventures to suggest that Farrer was the twentieth century's 'subtlest and most eloquent Anglican thinker'.[8] In a collection of brief biographies and reviews, the philosopher Anthony Kenny implies something very similar. Kenny wrote his own doctoral thesis on Farrer's philosophical theology; he confesses that each time he returns to Farrer's first book, *Finite and Infinite* (Farrer, 1943), he remains uncertain as to whether he has yet fully appreciated the entire argument.

One further stimulus on the occasion of the 2019 conference at Keble was the discovery of the four unpublished lectures given by him in Dallas and elsewhere in the USA in 1966, just two years before his death. Here, once again, the remarkable integrity and variety within his thought and his capacity to contribute across the boundaries within theological studies are notable. Increased specialisation in this past half century has made such an approach more problematic. These lectures, however, suggest that this cross-fertilisation and interaction may still offer an important corrective to the sometimes myopic concentration within theological disciplines.

So many of the issues upon which he focuses remain current. One of the fascinations of Farrer's work is his confidence to proceed without the now universally assumed use of the intellectual apparatus of footnoting or endnoting and the subsequent clear reference to sources. Even in the process of editing these lectures, this has proved to offer powerful challenges. Our editorial response has been to remain true to Farrer's approach and for the most part to avoid adding our own references, despite our reduced confidence in contrast to that of Farrer. References have been added only where they might add clarity or help to demystify comments now made obscure by the passage of the five decades since the lectures were delivered.

These four unpublished lectures have been left to retain their original style, as delivered in the lecture room. Very few editorial changes have been made. One or two rare examples of a certain chauvinism have been lightly revised: despite a general unfailing modesty, Farrer was not entirely innocent of the sin of hubris. (He once noted, when asked if he had read a certain book, that he did not know it, but then reflected that he tended to write books rather than read too many of them.)

Some brief introductory notes on the four lectures follow. Understandably, remembering that these were delivered more than 50 years ago, the language remains in several respects 'exclusive'. We have left it so, in order not to interfere with Farrer's characteristic style: doubtless were he writing today he would have adhered to the sensitivities of a changing culture. The lectures follow in the order in which he appears to have delivered them.

1 *Something Has Died on Us: Can it be God?*

In reading these essays, one has to transpose oneself into the atmosphere and issues of the day. The 1960s were years of some intellectual and cultural upheaval, often leading to stimulating new thoughts and pathways, but also frequently in ways that abandoned previously assumed intellectual compass bearings. Theology was by no means immune to this and notably in a more or less rigorous adoption by some of Friedrich Nietzsche's talk of the 'Death of God'. A number of American writers engaged with this enterprise, sometimes accompanied by a celebration of a secularised society: Harvey Cox's *The Secular City* (Cox, 1965) is perhaps the best known example of this genre.

In Britain too, similar themes emerged, notably in the so-called 'South Bank Theology', emerging from the Anglican Diocese of

Southwark. Bishop John Robinson's *Honest to God* (Robinson, 1963) was its most celebrated publication, translated into numerous languages, selling over one million copies and remaining in print until this day. Robinson did not press for a 'Death of God' approach, but instead attempted to popularise the work of Rudolf Bultmann, Paul Tillich and Dietrich Bonhoeffer.

In America, others – including Thomas Altizer, Paul van Buren and William Hamilton[9] – extended this approach into a more radical critique of theology and religious language. Interestingly enough, a number of enthusiasts moved in the direction of 'non-realism', a path later trodden in Britain by Don Cupitt[10] and his disciples. Thomas Altizer receives particular focus in Farrer's lecture. He responds with a sharply argued philosophical critique, but sets this within the attractive narrative and dialogue style generally adopted in his sermons and much of his theological writing. A more accessible style is adopted here than that in his two early books of philosophical theology, *Finite and Infinite* (Farrer, 1943) and *The Freedom of the Will* (Farrer, 1958); instead there is a greater resonance with his later work in *Saving Belief* (Farrer, 1964b) and *Faith and Speculation* (Farrer, 1967).

This lecture suggests that Farrer would have made short work of the recent outpourings of the so-called 'New Atheists'. He dismissed what he describes as 'cosmic rationalism'; his philosophical writing here reflects a similar use of 'reason' to that encountered in the theological writings of Samuel Taylor Coleridge. Farrer is never flippant in his dismissal of others' arguments. Nonetheless, he spares little scorn for some of the cruder arguments that emerged in the decade within which he was writing. Interestingly enough – and Farrer would doubtless have seen the irony were he still around – 'Death of God Theology' has long since been archived as a historical phenomenon in reference volumes, dictionaries of theology and web references.

2   How Far is Christian Doctrine Reformable?

If in the first lecture Farrer is responding directly to a current phenomenon in terms of 'Death of God Theology', then in this second lecture there is even a sense of prescience. The next decade would see an upsurge of interest in precisely the focus captured in the above title. In Britain, Anglican theologians responded to this theme: from the Patristics direction emerged Maurice Wiles's *The Remaking of Christian Doctrine* (Wiles, 1974); later, the multi-author volume *The Myth of God Incarnate* (Hick, 1977) touched on similar themes. It is regrettable that those authors did not have this essay before them, with which to be challenged.

Farrer's answer to his own question is not simply a conservative closing of the door, indeed far from it. Instead he begins by exposing the weaknesses of propositionalism with regard both to revelation within Scripture and also truth within doctrinal statements. As ever, he is keen to use imagery as his way into the debate. He refers to the work of the Second Vatican Council, noting a more nuanced approach to 'infallibility', following the Council. Farrer was often counter-suggestive in dealing with Roman Catholicism (he had been brought up a Baptist; his father had been a minister). Here, however, Farrer is keen to indicate how the expression of doctrinal truths can be re-stated and re-thought in the context of changing cultures and in the face of new philosophical insights. He is more than sceptical of Rudolf Bultmann's existential theology with its embarkation point in a wider programme of 'demythologisation'. It is interesting, once again, to see how unfashionable most existential thought has become, both within and outside Christian theology. In an earlier volume, *Kerygma and Myth* (Bartsch and Fuller, 1961), Farrer had already responded to this trend both within contemporary German theology and beyond. Farrer is keen, here as elsewhere, to affirm the importance of the 'supernatural'. By this he refers not to the miraculous, but to the agency of God within our world alongside human agency.

3 Bultmann and All That

This lecture extends some of the argument outlined above into the realms of New Testament theology. Issues relating to demythologising reappear, but this time more particularly in relation to the historical roots of the Christian faith. Farrer notes what he describes as three prejudices in relation to Christianity and history. The first prejudice is that truth about man's (*sic*) spiritual nature and the way of his salvation cannot be pinned to historical facts; history may be important, but one cannot universalise from it. Second, the special presence of a divine person at the centre of a uniquely revelatory event cannot be accepted. Third is the prejudice against a divine person (he uses this term as shorthand and not in a docetic sense) acting miraculously.

Here again, Bultmann and his disciples are Farrer's main targets. Bultmann's desire to recast our understanding of the New Testament by dispensing with myth, offering an existential understanding both of Jesus and his message, lies at the heart.

Farrer is concerned to avoid the road towards various forms of reductionism. He describes Bultmann's approach as being rooted in a 'rationalistic historiography'. He points to Paul as the primary witness and the author of the earliest material in the New Testament. Farrer also reacts to the 'atomisation' of the biblical documents implied in the crudest methods of form-criticism. His own use of images and poetry and literary critical methods places him alongside the early proponents of redaction criticism, and this fits well with his rejection of the Q hypothesis. He touches upon issues current and alive in present scholarship in a creative manner.

4   Does Social Structure Bow to Christian Morals, or Vice Versa?

It is almost uncanny how these four lectures feel alive to subsequent theological debate. The very title of this lecture brings to mind the focus of both John Milbank's Radical Orthodoxy with its starting point in *Theology and Social Theory* (Milbank, 1990), and also the broad compass of the writings of Stanley Hauerwas pleading for no further collusion with social studies or society more widely. Farrer's question stands astride the questions they both ask. Here there are resonances with the first of these lectures, since he is clearly responding to the 'new morality' of the 1960s, captured particularly in Joseph Fletcher's *Situation Ethics* (Fletcher, 1966) and in the writings once again of Bishop John Robinson in Britain. Situation ethics is specifically mentioned, and Farrer spends much of the lecture debating the question of 'moral rules'. Although rules remain helpful, Farrer's starting point is with 'measureless respect for others' and 'seeing with God'.

Effectively, his argument directs us towards Aristotle and, although it is not spelt out in as many words, he points precisely in the direction of 'virtue ethics' which, following Alasdair MacIntyre's *After Virtue* (MacIntyre, 1981), once again became central to Christian moral thought. Farrer hints too at 'natural law' theory and points to common moral codes inter-relating across very different cultures. His friend C. S. Lewis's book *The Abolition of Man* (Lewis, 1944) makes the rare appearance in a direct reference.

Here, then, is a considered response by a philosophical theologian to issues that remain at the heart of Christian moral debate. Farrer is realistic and generous to those who have focused on 'situations', but he is equally serious about reminding his audience of the crucial significance of an objective anchorage point for the moral life, where rules will be useful, without them being the primary focus or starting point.

Epilogue

The sermon that closes the volume was delivered at a special choral evening service in Keble Chapel, immediately after the 2019 conference. It uses the same discipline employed by Farrer, inasmuch as it takes as its starting point the set readings for that evening in the lectionary. It happened that one of these was the story of Cain's murder of his brother; and the other an extract from the Gospel According to St Matthew including two controversies between Jesus and successively the Pharisees and the Sadducees.

The story of Cain offers the sort of trope with which Farrer would frequently like to toy, using the imagery as the prompt for some deeper reflection on the nature of this Gospel. Here, themes of humanity's fallen nature and the need for redemption are effectively rehearsed. Farrer's Bampton Lectures, *The Glass of Vision*,[11] focus on the nature of revelation and the seminal role played by controlling images within that process. One of the key passages from those lectures, speaking directly to the question of revelation and poetic imagery, is quoted briefly in the sermon. The Gospel passage is also mentioned in the light of Farrer's approach.

Sermons focusing in this way were at the heart of Farrer's preaching which could remarkably speak to people both of theological specialism and others without such training. Even his very brief homilies composed for early morning quiet celebrations of the Eucharist, and whimsically labelled by some as *Farrergraphs*, offered a similar approach. Again, his integrated theological reflection is there even in his homiletic writing.

Markus Bockmuehl
Stephen Platten
29 June 2019
St Peter and St Paul

Notes

1 This recent event at Keble succeeded a 2004 Oxford conference prompted by the centenary of Farrer's birth. Durham and various American venues have also hosted symposia on Farrer. For further treatments of Farrer's life and work, see Curtis, 1985; Loades and MacSwain, 2006; Slocum, 2007.

2 Notably in his famous article 'On Dispensing With Q' (Farrer, 1955).

3 Cf. e.g. Poirier and Peterson, 2015; Titley, 2010, and see Mark Goodacre's treatment below.

4 See e.g. Conti, 1995; Hebblethwaite, 2007; Hedley and Hebblethwaite, 2006; Kennedy, 2011.

5 Cf. Curtis, 1985, p. 168.

6 See e.g. Goulder, 1977–8, 1996, 1999; Goodacre, 1996, 2001, 2002. A substantial number of other scholars have in recent years offered support to this view with a greater or lesser degree of confidence.

7 Lewis dedicated his *Reflections on the Psalms* (Lewis, 1958) to Austin and Katharine Farrer, and also wrote the preface to Farrer's 1960 collection of homilies (Farrer, 1960b; US edition Farrer, 1960a); as Judith Wolfe shows below, he expressed admiration for several other of Farrer's works.

8 Williams, 2018, p. xiv.

9 See e.g. Altizer and Hamilton, 1966; Van Buren, 1963.

10 E.g. Cupitt, 1980, 1997.

11 Farrer, 1948; cf. the re-edition with commentary by MacSwain, 2013.

PART ONE

Farrer at Keble –
The Gospels, C. S. Lewis
and Philosophical Theology

Austin Farrer as Warden of Keble (1960–1968)

IAN W. ARCHER

The Fellows of Keble were hardly enthusiastic supporters of Austin Farrer, then serving as Fellow and Chaplain of Trinity College, Oxford, when they put his name forward for the Wardenship in 1960 in succession to Eric Abbott, the recently appointed Dean of Westminster. According to the statutes the Warden was formally nominated by the Archbishop of Canterbury in his capacity as College Visitor assisted by two assessors, but in practice a nomination required the support of the Fellows who were allowed to deliberate on possible candidates. Archbishop Geoffrey Fisher had already indicated his support for Farrer in preliminary soundings in October 1959. Farrer had just been passed over for the Regius Chair of Divinity in favour of Henry Chadwick. Although he enjoyed the powerful advocacy of his fellow Metaphysicals (a club of Oxford philosophers) Basil Mitchell, he was scarcely known to the Fellowship, and several had serious misgivings, especially the Bursar Vere Davidge and the classicist Spencer Barrett, and more tentatively Douglas Price, Denys Potts and Dennis Shaw, tutors in History, French and Physics respectively. There was no doubting Farrer's scholarly credentials, but his abilities as an administrator were suspect. The other frontrunners were G. M. Styler, precentor of Corpus Christi Cambridge, and the youthful Dennis Nineham, then Professor of Divinity at King's College, London, and the man destined to be Farrer's successor at Keble. Douglas Price confided to his diary that 'Styler was safe but unexciting, Nineham exciting but dangerous, Farrer undoubtedly the strongest claimant as a scholar but doubtful as regards personality. I cannot believe the Church of England is so utterly destitute of men with both the humour and intellectual qualifications requisite in a Warden as has been protested.' At the straw poll of members of the Governing Body on 27 January 1960, there were six votes for Farrer, four for Styler and one for Nineham; when it came down to a choice between Farrer and Styler, the voting was just 6:5 in favour of Farrer. Price thought it culpable that Leonard Rice-Oxley, Fellow in English and Sub-Warden, did not tell the Archbishop the narrowness of the margin of victory, 'a piece of political chicanery more to be expected of a town council than a Governing Body meeting'. Farrer was duly nominated by the Archbishop.[1]

We are unusually well informed about this election, even to the extent of knowing who voted for whom, not because the Governing Body minutes tell us – they are characteristically reticent on the matter – but because Douglas Price, an old boy, Fellow in History since 1949, and the College's long-serving Dean, kept an unusually full diary. The diary is not one of the twentieth century's greatest literary productions – there is much that is mundane and trivial, and it's particularly informative on the weather; it was also the work of a pretty conservative bachelor don committed to a vision of the College that was at odds with the forces transforming British society in the 1960s. Typical is Price's remark that allowing undergraduates to entertain women guests at all meals was 'another stage in the destruction of the College's character as an academic society'.[2] He regretted the expansion of the College under Farrer, complaining shortly after his death that the 'headlong process' of expanding the Fellowship had 'disastrous consequences': 'they [the Fellows] have neither the willingness nor the ability to play their part in the government of the College; they ignore their social obligations; the relations with the junior members have steadily deteriorated as the dons have hidden behind committees . . . It is all very depressing to anyone who remembers the happiness and sense of unity which characterised the College in former days.'[3] It is a profoundly dyspeptic account.

At no point does Price acknowledge Farrer's significant published output; he exemplified the curious anti-intellectualism characteristic of the darker corners of the collegiate university. But his diary does tell us a lot about Farrer's tenure as Warden and the community he presided over. Although we need at times to read it against the grain, it is a major source for the account that follows, and it helps us to contextualise the rather dry formal records of the period. There are some memoirs of Fellows from this period: Basil Mitchell, a strong supporter at the outset, remained appreciative of Farrer's qualities; John Carey, tutor in English from 1960 to 1964 and an occupant of the flat above the Lodgings, was immensely impressed both by his intellect and by his ability to face down the more fractious members of the Governing Body; but Dennis Shaw, an early opponent, scarcely mentions Farrer at all, reminding us of the sometimes self-serving nature of such memoirs, already contaminated by hindsight.[4] The memoirs are in any case over-generalised and lack the granularity of Price's day-by-day account which sheds light on episodes such as the highly contentious election of Richard Hawkins as philosophy tutor in 1968, where the memory of witnesses falters, and which we might not otherwise know about.

In the satirical verse of which he was fond, Farrer joked about the degree to which his powers as Warden were circumscribed:

A seventh Warden reigns where Talbot sat,
Reigns but not rules; the Fellows saw to that.[5]

It is notable that when the College set up its key standing committees – Bursarial, Senior Tutors, and Buildings – in 1966 it was decided that the Warden should not be an elected member of any of them, and although he might attend them, he would not displace the usual Chairman.[6] Farrer himself claimed that the position of a head of college 'has two consequences – first, that being a constitutional monarch he can only achieve his aims by intrigue which takes a disproportionate amount of doing; second, that it being assumed that his time is of no value, he has to volunteer for trifling tasks'.[7] Sure enough, in December 1966 Farrer was personally involved in 'Operation Joshua', helping to move books from the Upper Library to the newly opened book stack.[8] But, as we shall see, we need to take some of this self-deprecation with a pinch of salt. Farrer's role was undoubtedly greater than often claimed.

Farrer was undoubtedly uncomfortable with some of the more public aspects of his role as Warden. Moving though his sermons might have been, the chapel acoustic was unfriendly to his mode of delivery. Price described his inauguration sermon as 'somewhat mystical, finely phrased but unimpressively delivered'.[9] Speeches on formal occasions often misfired. His first address to the freshers was a 'confused harangue' about the timing of chapel services; his speech at the retirement dinner of the long-serving Chemistry don G. D. Parkes in 1965 was 'as rambling as ever'; he got muddled at gaudies, on one occasion with 250 MAs present forgetting to propose the toast to the health of the College.[10] Price claimed that he made a 'fetish of informality', but sometimes with unfortunate results, as when he instructed Archbishop Ramsey not to reply when the College drank his health in 1963.[11]

The Lodgings had reverted to the austerity of decoration characteristic of Harry Carpenter's time (Abbott had apparently livened things up),[12] but Farrer could be a generous host, and there were memorable dinner parties in the Lodgings. Social occasions had an added edge because Farrer's wife, Katharine (née Newton), the detective novelist, was 'so neurotic you imagined she'd emit a shower of sparks if placed in a dark room'.[13] Price nevertheless recalls an agreeable occasion in 1963 when the Farrers entertained Kathleen Major, the Principal of St Hilda's and the distinguished ancient historian Fergus Millar and his wife, as well as some of the Keble Fellows; the young English don John Carey enjoyed a memorable dinner with C. S. Lewis, a close friend of the Farrers.[14] But Farrer was ill at ease in entertaining undergraduates: Price complained early on that he had abandoned his predecessor's sherry parties; perhaps he preferred other methods, but Roger

Boden recalls a tea party of 'excruciating awkwardness'.[15] It looks like he avoided student societies like the Mitre Club (a chapel-orientated society) whose dinner he attended only twice in 1963 and 1965.[16] Price had fretted during his first term that Farrer might confine his pastoral attentions to the ordinands and although that does not seem to have been the case, he does not seem to have been a very powerful presence within the undergraduate body. Very few of the student memoirs gathered in the early 1990s recall him, though Tim Faithfull, a JCR (Junior Common Room) President, remembers him as 'intense and rather shy though capable of great excitement when urging on the Keble boat in Eights Week', which if true is a significant revision to the received wisdom.[17] Farrer also had contact with undergraduates through his involvement in the teaching of Theology and Philosophy.

Farrer's role as Warden was complicated by his own position as a priest and the expectation that he would play a full role in the life of the chapel. The signs are that he was very closely involved though his relationship with the Chaplain, Christopher Stead, remains somewhat opaque. He had an ability to 'extemporise in Prayer Book English with extraordinary facility', producing numerous collects of his own.[18] Chapel services continued to offer an austere version of Anglo-Catholicism – there had been no incense since the days of Warden Kidd – but the Eucharist (still scheduled for 8.30 am on Sundays and the main service of the week) included *sotto voce* additions in Latin, not calculated to appeal to evangelicals for whom, in spite of his nonconformist upbringing, Farrer had little time.[19] But other changes seem to have alienated mainstream Anglicans like Price who saw the moves in the direction of greater informality in a very negative light: 'The Warden has deprived this service of all its former dignity without giving it the alternative virtue of simplicity. Seats are placed across the chancel, the choir no longer in surplices, Mrs Farrer occupying the Warden's stall; the music was abominable.'[20] Although the proportion of Anglican Fellows was declining, Farrer was determined to involve them in the life of the chapel, and encouraged them to take communion on the first Sunday of term. This initiative enjoyed a modest success, with usually at least six, and on one occasion as many as ten Fellows present.[21] He also introduced a termly corporate communion which seems to have boosted chapel attendances (its Sunday evening timing helped), and he encouraged the use of the chapel by students of St Anne's whose members began to sing in the choir from 1968.[22] The Warden interviewed all freshers during their first term, and one of the more remarkable survivals from his tenure is the album with their photos and Farrer's notes on their religious affiliations. In 1962, 72 of the 102 freshmen declared themselves to be members of the Church of England, though of these eight were lapsed or non-communicant, and six were unconfirmed. In addition to the Anglicans there was a sprinkling of nonconformists – six Methodists, three Presbyterians, one Congregationalist, and one simply nonconformist. Three he described as 'papists', and there was one Orthodox and one Lutheran. Only two declared themselves to be of 'no religion'.[23]

The College was not immune to the growing student radicalism of the 1960s, though one has the sense of rather distant ripples from major events further away. Student demands occasionally reflected international political causes but more often focused on the easing of the disciplinary regime and its adaptation to changing mores, but the Governing Body was pretty resistant to change. A request for a boycott of South African goods in 1960. Refused. A request to install a TV in the JCR in 1960. Refused. A request to abolish the requirement that scholars sit at a separate table at Hall in 1963. Refused. A request that men should not have to take lunch in College. Refused. A request to extend the hours of entertainment of women guests to 11.30 pm in 1965. Refused.[24] It did give way gradually and grudgingly. The JCR got their TV as a reward for winning *University Challenge* in 1964, though they had to wait for the cigarette vending machine until 1968; the scholars' table was eventually abandoned after student walk outs; female guests were increasingly welcome at JCR guest nights (up to four a term from 1966); in November 1966 tentative moves for consulting with students were instigated; there were moves to greater transparency in the disciplinary processes.[25] But there were real limits to the changes. A committee to consider relations between junior and senior members in June 1968 – a rather sensitive period in student activism internationally – was expressly forbidden to take evidence from students. Demands for formal student representation on the Governing Body were rebuffed, though at the last Governing Body before Farrer's death the College established the so-called Senior Liaison Committee comprising the Sub Warden, Bursar, Dean, Senior Tutor, and the Senior Treasurers of the Amalgamated Clubs who were to meet twice a term with student representatives.[26]

As for Farrer's contribution to the administration of the College, we have to make allowances both for his self-deprecating style and for the tendency of the Fellows to magnify their own roles, especially in retrospect. There is no doubting his energy. Everyone testifies to his running about College (the undergraduates dubbed him 'the White Rabbit'; Carey describes him as 'lean, quick and witty'); or how terrifying it was to be driven by him in his car. Basil Mitchell tells us that he proved to be an excellent administrator; even Price conceded that he presided efficiently and expeditiously at College meetings, though it is striking that they regularly ran on for as long as three hours. He did get involved in the minutiae, intervening for example in some of the trickier cases of the College's ecclesiastical patronage.[27] Interestingly both Price and Mitchell agree that he was sometimes impetuous. Mitchell says that 'his only fault . . . was that he reached decisions too rapidly or at least before his colleagues had caught up with him. He seemed always to be several moves ahead of us.' Or as Price put it at the College's alumni dinner in London very soon after his death

when he came to preside over meetings of the Governing Body, he was always seeking to cut through the knots of debate to get a quick decision – to make time for something else; and he was too honest to disguise the irritation which he sometimes justly felt at the preciosity on the one hand or the verbosity on the other of some of our utterances on these occasions. There were times when we felt as if we were running desperately behind the chariot of Jehu, picking up the bits along the road. But the chariot never came to grief, and looking back the exercise did us good.[28]

Farrer, it has to be said, was no naïf, and he was under no illusions as to the foibles of his new colleagues. According to Adrian Darby he was 'deeply religious, fastidious, highly intelligent, and at times as maliciously waspish as a saint is allowed to be'.[29] The Fellows, needless to say, could be fractious. Sometimes Farrer himself was the object of criticism. In January 1966 both Davidge and Spencer Barrett were outraged by the Warden's unilateral reduction of a disciplinary sentence of rustication, but Farrer defused it by 'putting on a white sheet' at the subsequent College Meeting.[30] Any college that harboured a personality as overpowering as Cecil Vere Davidge, Fellow in Law since 1931, and Bursar from 1948 until 1968, was going to pose challenges. Davidge was purportedly as hostile to intellectual values as he was passionate about rowing, and he combined his role as College Fellow with the life of a country gentleman; he was an active member of the Pytchley Hunt and a former High Sheriff of Northamptonshire. The portrait that he presented to the College on his retirement shows him in hunting pink with a glass of port in hand. Although he became a caricature of himself, he was no fool and a formidable operator whose support was usually essential to progress business, but he could also be disruptive.[31] When he stood up for one of his protégés who had been implicated in Boat Club disorders, an uncomfortable College Meeting followed at which members accused each other of discourtesy.[32] As John Carey, admittedly a hostile witness, memorably puts it, 'confronting Davidge at governing body meetings . . . Farrer was . . . needle-sharp, every particle of his being a living quivering reproach to what Davidge represented'.[33] But Davidge was not the only source of tension. The classicist Spencer Barrett, though committed to make things work (he delighted in the details of salary scales, and undertook the redesign of the Porter's Lodge in 1962), was sensitive on points where the College's clerical character might be brought into the open: as a committed atheist he had been unable to take up his Fellowship until the change in statutes in 1952.[34] And as the decade advanced, many of the new appointments adopted an aggressive stance on the issues of the day. Paul Hayes, appointed as Fellow in Politics in 1967, made an early impact for his trademark outspokenness.[35] Things became more turbulent towards the end of Farrer's tenure. Davidge's increasingly erratic behaviour – his boorish antics at High Table were notorious – antagonised several of the younger Fellows, and his attempt in 1967 to get his Fellowship extended three years beyond the retirement age as allowed by the very statute he had drafted in 1952 met with stiff resistance, and on this occasion the 'Young Turks' (led by Paul Hayes and Alec Campbell) had the Warden's support. In the event Davidge was assuaged with his election to an Honorary Fellowship – Price takes the credit for this compromise – though apparently the Bursar went round telling the undergraduates that he had been sacked; perhaps that backfired because a group of them showed their feelings by hanging him in effigy, port glass in hand, from one of the Library gargoyles a few months later.[36]

Academics are notoriously fickle in their appreciation of the quality of their leaders. Farrer was not as sociable as Eric Abbott and that damned him in the eyes of the traditionalists like Price. The collective memory also tends to telescope the historical process and focuses on tangible results. So Keble has tended to celebrate the achievements of the 1970s and 1980s in terms of new buildings and improved academic standards, and Farrer's successors, Dennis Nineham and Christopher Ball, have taken the credit. But the truth is that the essential foundations of those successes were laid under Farrer.[37]

It is true that Keble's academic standing remained poor, not helped by Davidge's policy of shoeing in Etonian oarsmen, 'worthless clots', 'ignorant louts better qualified for employment as navvies', according to the jaundiced Price.[38] Keble enjoyed sporting success – it was Head of the River in 1963,

1967 and 1968, and the enthusiasm for rowing was infectious with Keble putting ten boats on the river in 1966, but this came at an academic price, and its students performed well below University averages. In the mid-1960s 57% of its arts students secured Firsts or Seconds compared to the University average of 68%; the scientists performed rather better with 64% taking Firsts or Seconds compared to the University average of 72%. The College remained stubbornly near the bottom of the Norrington Table which recorded college rankings throughout the decade. Another unfortunate consequence was that there was a palpable social division between the grammar school-boys and the public school men. No fewer than 38 Etonians were admitted between 1960 and 1965, 5.5% of the student total; there were many others from other rowing schools like Shrewsbury and Radley.[39] The postgraduate body was skewed towards those reading diplomas rather than research degrees; in 1964 Balliol had 22 Rhodes scholars, and Keble none.[40] The College's ability to improve was limited by its relatively poor financial standing. It was not among the very poorest of the colleges, but it was pretty poor, and the lower remuneration offered to Fellows was sufficient to cause John Carey to move to St John's as soon as the opportunity presented itself.[41]

But the winds of change were stirring. It was an age of reform in the wider University. Oxford's curricula and its examination systems were being questioned as the pressure for wider participation in higher education grew. It was an uncomfortable time for colleges whose admissions procedures and teaching methods were beginning to come under critical scrutiny. A variety of internal committees tackled reform piecemeal, dealing with matters such as admissions (Hardie committee, 1962), and syllabuses (Kneale committee, 1965). The government-appointed Robbins committee of 1961–63 was a real wake-up call, much more confrontational, criticising the scholarship and entrance system as undermining the university sector as a whole, noting the narrowness of Oxford recruitment (70% of places went to candidates from the public schools), and expressing the need for an expansion of postgraduate education.[42] In 1964–65 the

University's administration, teaching and research were scrutinised by an internal public commission of inquiry under the chairmanship of Oliver Franks, set up to head off a royal commission. Its recommendations set out to adapt the collegiate ideal for the modern world, requiring the reform of admissions processes and academic appointments, while shifting the balance of power between the colleges and central University organs. It did not in fact effect a revolution, as Congregation blocked some of the more radical proposals, but it undoubtedly contributed to the shift in the terms of public discourse within the collegiate University.[43]

The character of Keble was indeed changing rapidly. Student numbers had begun to surge forwards: the head count was 292 in 1955, 372 in 1960, and 430 in 1970. In terms of its undergraduate numbers Keble was the second largest of the colleges by 1970. Expansion in postgraduate numbers from 28 to 72 was particularly marked in the 1960s; the Middle Common Room was inaugurated in 1964; just before Farrer's death the College agreed to two postgraduate awards to be offered in open competition with stipends of £100 per annum and limited dining rights.[44] The Fellowship was expanding and diversifying: Farrer inherited a Governing Body of 11 Fellows; by the time of his death there were 27. Times were favourable for expansion because of the pressure from the University for colleges to take on the 'non-dons', research scientists who currently lacked College Fellowships; hence expansion could occur at relatively little cost. The College's first posts in Mathematics, Engineering, Medicine and Biochemistry came under Farrer's tenure, and by 1970 32% of undergraduates were reading for science subjects. But there were also Fellowships for the first time in non-science subjects such as German, Music and Politics.[45] It was another sign of the times that when G. D. Parkes stood down after long service as Senior Tutor, his place was taken by an energetic reformer, the historian Eric Stone in 1965. Although Davidge may have been a joke as a tutor, he had a shrewd eye for talent, ensuring the appointment of David Williams, Peter North and Dyson Heydon as his colleagues: to have spotted talented future vice-chancellors of Cambridge and Oxford and an Australian High Court Justice was no mean feat. He was also behind the candidacy of the well-connected (married to Alec Douglas-Home's daughter) and rather clever Adrian Darby for the post in Economics.[46] It is hard to measure these things (there was no REF (Research Excellence Framework)[47]), but there appears to have been a ramping up of the intellectual quality of the Fellowship (significantly unremarked by Price!): in addition to those already named, the College made appointments of the calibre of John Carey, Malcolm Parkes, Raoul Franklin, Jim Griffin and Adrian Hollis, in English, Palaeography, Engineering, Philosophy and Classics respectively. Carey has recorded his shock therapy tactics in attempting to raise academic standards in English.[48] In 1965 Spencer Barrett became the first serving fellow to become a Fellow of the British Academy; Farrer's followed in 1968. It is true that Farrer was not necessarily comfortable with all the changes to the College over which he presided, fearing that it was selling out to 'industrial interests . . . that it would be turned over to engineering and business management with a little commercial Spanish'. He expressed the hope that the non-science Fellows who were still in a majority would 'rally around the Ark of the Covenant and lay down a line to hold Natural Sciences to 33%'.[49]

Whatever his misgivings about some aspects of the academic agenda, Farrer clearly recognised the need for new buildings. Apart from the small extension on the north Liddon range, the Besse Building opened in 1956 in the Butterfield idiom, the College estate was essentially as Butterfield had left it in the 1880s. The College was therefore able to house only a diminishing proportion of its undergraduates; its Library was now too cramped; the facilities for Fellows were inadequate to the increasing size of the teaching body. And the fabric was in poor shape: dry rot infested the Hall roof; everywhere there was crumbling masonry and brickwork. During the harsh winter of 1962–3 large sections of the parapet of the Liddon east range crashed to the ground (ominously on the day of the archbishop's visitation); the statue of St Michael on the chapel roof had to be replaced in 1967.[50] In addition to this seemingly interminable work of patching and mending, there were some significant new projects. The boat house, a shared facility with Jesus College, was opened in 1964 to nautically inspired designs by Z. W. Nirrenski.[51] In 1966 the College cleared away the outbuildings, boiler houses, and the remains of the so-called *cloaca maxima* (the original student toilets) between the Hall-Library block and the Clock Tower to make way for an expansion of the SCR (Senior Common Room) and the building of the Library book stack to designs by Messrs Alan Stubbs and partners.[52] Financial considerations seem to have caused significant delays to both these projects; the boat house had required a large bank loan, and it was clear that the pressing need for student accommodation could not be addressed without significant fund raising. The omens were not good. Farrer's Wardenship had opened with an unexpected rebuff from the Oxford Historic Buildings Appeal to whom an application for £25,000 had been made: apparently the buildings were not old enough. There was a flurry of protest in the press, but to no avail.[53]

Farrer was not an obvious natural for fund raising. On meeting an alumnus who claimed to have an entrée to an American millionaire, he opined: 'There is no business to which noblesse does not oblige, and I am now a great Lord.'[54] Among those he would have dealt with was one Captain Robert Maxwell whose Pergamon Press funded Keble's first graduate scholarship from 1962 (interestingly for someone from an undergraduate science background to study humanities, an attempt to bridge C. P. Snow's two cultures); Maxwell, by now a Labour MP, was also consulted about the appeal in December 1967 and apparently made a good impression.[55] Farrer had made several academic visits to the USA as a guest lecturer – at Yale in 1961, New York in 1964, and Texas and Louisiana in 1966 – but when it came to the serious fund raising mission to the States in 1968, he backed down on the grounds of ill health and Dennis Shaw was sent instead, but Farrer had done a considerable amount of the preparatory work, including writing letters to prospective donors.[56] He fastidiously approached fund raising as an ethical matter, writing a paper for the Governing Body in November 1963, which addressed the qualms 'felt among us about the morality or perhaps the decency of an appeal'. He fretted about the problem of donor-led philanthropy: 'we must not get into a false position by adopting objectives which happen to be money catching; we'd better make up our minds about what we really want to be'.[57] But for all this, there was a significant ramping up of the appeal strategy under his Wardenship.

The College had in fact already launched an appeal fund in 1951 on the initiative of a devoted alumnus Dick Walters. Ten years later it had raised a paltry £12,000, and a revised target figure of £250,000 for the centenary of 1970 was set.[58] The scope of the College's ambitions steadily widened, though progress was painfully slow. In 1963 it was proposed to create a major centenary fund to put up new buildings and endow fellowships.[59] There were indications of an increasingly professional approach as the consultants Hooker, Craigmyle and Co. were approached in 1962. Although they were kept at arm's length, Dr Douglas V. Reid, a clerical tycoon allegedly with strong links to potential donors, acquired considerable influence over meetings of the Appeal Committee. Price observed these developments with predictable distaste: Reid, he thought, was 'a bounder but no doubt an able one'.[60] Efforts concentrated on the alumni base at first; there was a reluctance to approach business as the time never seemed right. There were false starts like a lottery scheme proposed by one of the College's more dubious North American contacts in 1967 (Farrer seems to have torpedoed that one!),[61] and the approach to American Episcopal universities for an exchange student scheme, backed by a financial package (an initiative Farrer was keen on, and which went forward after his death on a limited basis).[62] There was also some fuzziness over what the objectives of the campaign should be: 'much vague and inconclusive talk about a College appeal: when will the body make up its mind?' whined Price in November 1963. Two years later, he declared: 'it almost seems as if after three years we may be about to do something positive', before adding with a dash of his characteristic pessimism, 'having waited until the economic situation is as unpromising for an appeal as can be'. But a permanent organisation for the Centenary Fund was established at the end of 1965 and the appeal brochure sent out with a covering letter from Farrer to the alumni throughout the world.[63] A network of regional contacts was established and they were sent a booklet on how to make approaches to possible donors; sherry parties were arranged at various locations around the country: Price was dispatched to Liverpool, Norwich, Edinburgh, and the Bishop of Worcester's residence at Hartlebury Castle.[64] This was accompanied by significant work on building design. In 1966 Sir Hugh Casson, Conder and Partners were brought in as development consultants on what was known as the Keble College Development Plan (the first of many), which appeared the following year, identifying the Museum Road, Blackhall Road site (the so-called southern option, preserving the Fellows' Garden) as suitable for new accommodation. A colour brochure now extended the funding priorities beyond the immediate needs for the extension to the Senior Common Room and the new Library book stack to new undergraduate accommodation; the aim was now to extend the appeal beyond alumni to businesses and educational trusts, though this was postponed until 1968 because of the economic climate.[65] In October 1968 Shaw embarked on his North American tour, and with £220,000 pledged by the time of Farrer's death in December 1968, the College set a new target of £1 million, of which it was hoped half would be received by the centenary in June 1970. This was impressive progress.[66]

Still more important for the future was the fact that through the good offices of Kenneth Mills, an alumnus, and the charm of Adrian Darby whose shared enthusiasm for art tweaked the benefactor's interest, the College had established contact with Andre de Breyne (then chairman of Pearsons), who had agreed to give £50,000 on condition that the College found match-ing funds within a year. Although only £30,000 was secured (from the Rank Organisation Charitable Trust), de Breyne was sufficiently impressed that he fulfilled his pledge to the full – this news came a few days before Farrer's death.[67] It was the beginning of a relationship with transformative effects for the College. Another large donation of £42,600 came from the Revd Hiram Kennedy Douglass (1893–1975), another North American clerical tycoon who had fond memories of his time at Keble under Warden Kidd just after the First World War.[68] By 1971 at the end of the centenary year the appeal had reached a total of £418,000. After considering 14 possible architects, the Governing Body approved the appointment of Ahrends, Burton and Koralek on 27 November 1968.[69] Thus at Farrer's death all the elements were in place to allow the College to proceed with the ABK Building, the most significant addition to the estate since the Victorian era.

A dark shadow over the fundraising campaign was the question of identity: what was the College for? Its clerical origins seemed much less relevant as the number of ordinands plummeted (only 8% went on to careers in the Church by the end of the 1950s compared to 36% in the inter war period) and the student body diversified with the addition of new subjects.[70] The 1952 statutes had removed the require-ment that the Fellows be members of the Church of England, and had made the College fully self-governing, dissolving the Council of externals, a body of lay and clerical worthies that had increasingly seemed to stand in the way of change. There was little sign of embarrassment about the College's origins in the commemoration of the centenary of John Keble's death, marked by an exhibition in the spring of 1966 attended by 1,300 people.[71] But the ghosts of the College's clerical past had not been laid to rest, and the 'Young Turks' seemed at times to be spoiling for a fight.[72]

Farrer's sincerely articulated confessional position at times threatened to conjure them forth. Even Price suspected him of using a BBC documentary about the College presented by John

Betjeman (an Honorary Fellow), which appeared in November 1968, to push the College's clerical character.[73] More ominous was the major row over the Philosophy post to replace Basil Mitchell on his promotion to a university chair at Oriel College in the same year. Farrer wanted a Christian philosopher in Mitchell's mould rather than Richard Hawkins, an old member who had been encouraged to apply, the preferred candidate of Jim Griffin (a recent appointment in philosophy) and the arch-sceptic on religious matters, Spencer Barrett. Price was shocked to learn that Farrer had failed to consult with Griffin, and a major confrontation at Governing Body loomed. Farrer was pretty dug in, claiming that Hawkins was 'actively antichristian', and Price feared that positions had become so polarised that the Visitor might have to be called in. It was on this occasion that Price records his most damning indictment of Farrer who, he claimed, had lost all sense of proportion. 'Surely his election to be Warden was one of the major disasters of the College's history.' In the event Farrer backed down in the face of pretty overwhelming opposition from the Fellows, adopting the face-saving formula that the College had some obligation to Hawkins having encouraged him to apply.[74] But for many the issue focused the continuing anomaly in the statutes (which had been a compromise) that the Warden should be in holy orders. It is striking that within days of Farrer's tragic death on 29 December 1968 the Fellows, now under the inter-regnal leadership of the atheist Spencer Barrett as Vice-Warden, moved to get the statutes revised to remove the requirement. On 22 January 1969 a straw vote among the Fellows indicated strong support for the removal of the clerical requirement; 19 were in favour, six against, with two abstentions.[75]

Farrer remained true to an ideal he had set out in a letter written to his father in 1928, in which he asserted that 'you cannot research profitably into the philosophy of religion . . . until you know what you are talking about and the sphere to reveal that to you is the practical life'.[76] We have seen how regularly those who encountered him described him as a saint, with the implication that he was not quite of this world. But in

his address at the memorial service Basil Mitchell downplayed
the other-worldliness of Farrer. He was

> quite unlike the sort of academic who thinks but cannot
> act. Thought with him was incipient action . . . He was
> not in the least remote from the world in which cabbages
> are grown, furniture mended, roofs inspected and drains
> cleared. In another sense perhaps he *was* unworldly. He was
> almost entirely indifferent to and largely unaffected by the
> world in which reputations are made, movements initiated,
> influences received or imparted. Using the word broadly he
> had no *political* interests. It was difficult to get him to take
> seriously the organised activities of any body intermediate
> between the college and the cosmos. It was entirely natural
> that in one of his most memorable sermons he should have
> maintained that the City of God was really a collection of
> villages. He might almost have said 'colleges'.[77]

There is no doubting his devotion to the community of which
he became part in 1960, and the practical wisdom he brought
to its affairs. Farrer has perhaps suffered in the College's collective memory because he lacked the bonhomie which characterised his predecessor and successor, and because in the
College's dominant narrative of 'improvement', it is the 1970s
and 1980s which have attracted our attention. But in terms of
the key initiatives and relationships which laid the foundations
for those successes we need to look to Farrer's tenure.

Notes

1 The Douglas Price (1915–99) diaries run from 1935 during
his second year as an undergraduate to September 1999. The Keble
College call numbers are KC/AD 37 1/1 to KC/AD 37 1/187. They
have been referred to in the notes as simply Diary, with entries identified by date. For Farrer's election, see Diary, 29.7.1959, 30.7.1959,
14.10.1959, 18.10.1959, 28.10.1959, 18.11.1959, 26.11.1959,
2.12.1959, 16.1.1960, 18.1.1960, 27.1.1960, 6.2.1960. Other

candidates considered who seem to have been eliminated at an earlier stage included Kenneth Woolcombe, then Chaplain of St John's College Oxford and later Bishop of Oxford, and Carlyle Witton-Davies, the recently appointed Archdeacon of Oxford. For the statutes of 1952, which governed the formal process, see KC/GOV1 A1/23. For an outline of Farrer's career, see Crombie, 2004; for an appreciation of his intellectual significance see Mascall, 1978.

2 Diary, 16.10.1968.

3 Diary, 23.6.1969.

4 KC/AD 32/2, 'Reminiscences of Basil Mitchell. Life as a Keble Don'; Carey, 2014; KC2017/24, 'Memoirs of Dennis Frederick Shaw'.

5 Curtis, 1985, p. 157.

6 KC/GOV 1 C3/5 (Governing Body minutes, 1966–1972), 26.10.1966.

7 Curtis, 1985, p. 156.

8 Curtis, 1985, pp. 159–60; The Record, 1967, p. 5.

9 Diary, 9.10.1960.

10 Diary, 8.10.1960, 25.4.1962, 25.6.1965.

11 Diary, 27.1.1963.

12 Diary, 7.10.1960.

13 Carey, 2014, 175.

14 Diary, 14.3.1963; Carey, 2014, pp. 178–9.

15 Diary, 18.11.1960; Roger Boden, personal information.

16 Diary, 10.5.1963, 14.5.1965.

17 Diary, 18.11.1960; KC/MEM 2 D3/1, 1956–65, memoir of Tim Faithfull. Others claim he was 'an eccentric character who seemed more or less a recluse'; alternatively, 'a man whose saintly qualities I have come to recognise subsequently through his writings'; ibid. 1966–75, memoir of Tony Thomson; 1956–65, memoir of Richard Brown. Needless to say, student recollections of Vere Davidge, on whom more below, were rather more vivid.

18 Curtis, 1985, p. 162.

19 Curtis, 1985, p. 162; Diary, 26.4.1967 for lack of incense since 1939.

20 Diary, 15.1.1961, 10.11.1968.

21 Diary, 14.10.1962.

22 Curtis, 1985, pp. 158–9; Diary, 15.1.1967, 5.3.1967, 23.4.1967.

23 KC/MEM 2 C1/2.

24 KC/GOV1 C3/4 (Governing Body minutes, 1951–1966), 9.3.1960, 1.5.1963, 6.5.1964, 10.11.1965.

25 KC/GOV1 C3/4, 6.11.1963; 12.12.1964, 16.3.1966, KC/GOV1 C3/5, 9.11.1966, 23.11.1966, 21.6.1967, 27.11.1968; Diary, 6.6.1963; KC/MEM 2 D3/1, 1956–1965, memoir of T. C. Jobson.

26 KC/GOV 1 C3/5, 25.6.1968, 18.12.1968.

27 Diary, 22.2.1967, 11.11.1967, 27.11.1967.

28 Carey, 2014, p. 175; KC/AD 32/2, 'Reminiscences of Basil Mitchell', pp. 25–7; the bulk of Mitchell's eulogy at the memorial service is given in *The Record*, 1969, pp. 3–7; Douglas Price, 'Speech at Keble London Dinner', 7.1.1969, KC/WAR 7 D1-3.

29 Adrian Darby, personal information. Compare Carey, 2014, p. 177: Farrer was 'capable of asperity as saints no doubt need to be'.

30 Diary, 31.1.1966, 2.2.1966.

31 Cameron and Archer, 2008, p. 131.

32 Diary, 4.12.1965, 8.12.1965.

33 Carey, 2014, p. 179. Carey's account of Davidge at pp. 179–81 is a real skewering.

34 Hollis, 2001; Diary, 15.3.1967.

35 Diary, 20.4.1967, 21.2.1968.

36 Diary, 20.4.1967, 4.10.1967, 10.10.1967, 11.10.1967, 8.11.1967, 12.2.1968.

37 This intended as a swipe at Cameron and Archer, 2008!

38 Diary, 24.7.1963, 2.12.1964.

39 Cameron and Archer, 2008, 136–7; KC/MEM 2 D3/1, 1966–75, memoir of Ivor Roberts; data on admissions from Drennan, 1970.

40 Thomas, 1994, p. 214.

41 Dunbabin, 1994, p. 657; Carey, 2014, pp. 174–5.

42 *Robbins Report*, para. 687.

43 Halsey, 1994. Something of the impact of the successive enquiries can be seen in the admittedly patchy surviving correspondence files from Farrer's Wardenship: KC/WAR 7 A/12 (Robbins), A/14 (Franks). Price, ever the backwoodsman, complained regularly about the 'relentless', 'interminable', and 'cursed' questionnaires sent out by Franks, and claims that the commission was 'out of touch with realities'. Diary, 14.10.1964, 21.10.1964, 20.1.1965.

44 *The Record*, 1964, p. 3.

45 Cameron and Archer, 2008, pp. 133–4; see also *The Record*, 1965, pp. 17–18.

46 Diary, 7.3.1963.

47 Since 2014, the REF has been the system for assessing the quality of research in UK higher education institutions.

48 Carey, 2014, pp. 181–3.

49 Curtis, 1985, p. 156.

50 *The Record*, 1963, p. 3; 1967, pp. 2–3.

51 *The Record*, 1961, p. 18; 1964, p. 1.

52 *The Record*, 1964, pp. 1–2; 1966, pp. 5–6; 1967, pp. 4–5.

53 *The Record*, 1961, p. 3; Diary, 20.5.1961. This was the occasion of Farrer's comic ditty 'On the Rocks' posted in the SCR and reproduced in Curtis, 1985, pp. 157–8; KC/WAR 7 E/1–5.

54 Curtis, 1985, p. 133.

55 *The Record*, 1963, pp. 8–9; Diary, 22.12.1967.

56 Curtis, 1985, p. 158; 'Memoirs of Dennis Shaw'; Diary, 23.10.1968.

57 KC/WAR 7 A1/67, 'Warden Farrer's thoughts on the College Appeal'.

58 KC/GOV 1 C3/4, 17.10.1962.

59 KC/BF 7/8/1; KC/BF 7/8/2, KC/BF 7/8/3.

60 KC/GOV 1 C3/4, 6.11.1963, 20.11.1963; Diary, 15.10.1963, 11.10.1963, 19.10.1963, 2.2.1965, 20.5.1965, 4.11.1965, 3.3.1966.

61 Diary, 1.9.1967, KC/GOV 1 C3/5, 1.11.1967.

62 Diary, 4.10.1968, 30.10.1968; The Record, 1969, p. 10.

63 Diary, 6.11.1963, 4.11.1965; The Record, 1966, pp. 8–9.

64 Diary, 9.9.1966, 15.10.1966, 5.2.1967, 24.2.1967.

65 KC/GOV 1 C3/4, 23.3.1966, 8.6.1966, 27.7.1966, KC/GOV 1 C3/5, 12.10.1966, 15.2.1967; KC/BF 7/8/4; The Record, 1967, pp. 6–9.

66 The Record, 1969, pp. 14–15.

67 Diary, 28.11.1968, 3.12.1968.

68 The Record, 1969, pp. 14–17. For Douglass, whose contribution gets overlooked, see the Florence-Lauderdale Public Library Digital Archive, Who's Who in Old Florence, No. 27.

69 KC/GOV 1 C3/5, 15.5.1968; 27.11.1968.

70 The Record, 1965, pp. 18–19.

71 The Record, 1966, pp. 1–3.

72 Cf. Diary, 15.3.1967.

73 Diary, 7.7.1968, 14.11.1968.

74 Diary, 6.2.1968, 7.2.1968, 8.2.1968, 16.2.1968, 20.2.1968, 21.2.1968.

75 Diary, 9.1.1969, 22.1.1969; KC/GOV 1 C3/5, 9.1.1969, 18.1969, 22.1.1969.

76 Curtis, 1985, p. 54.

77 The Record, 1969, pp. 3–7.

Farrer and the Gospels

MARK GOODACRE

Farrer as a Biblical Scholar

A day after Austin Farrer's sudden and unexpected death on 29 December 1968, his obituary in *The Times* lamented that 'To the great disappointment of those who felt that Farrer's imaginative approach offered a refreshing way out of the sterile sands to which Form Criticism seemed to be leading, he was not appointed Regius Professor of Divinity in 1958'.[1] But the University's loss had been Keble's gain, and when he became Warden of the College in 1960, there was still a sense in the University's Faculty of Theology that Farrer's explorations in Biblical Studies were maverick, fanciful, and fell some way short of his true genius as a philosopher and a theologian. Students would be well advised to steer clear of his imaginative approach, in which the evangelists came alive as exciting authors of carefully coded narratives, and to keep their feet firmly on the ground of the safe and sober post-war consensus that retained an emphasis on the Gospels as patchworks of prior traditions.

But now, 50 years after his death, Farrer's inspirational New Testament scholarship is appreciated in a way that would have surprised his detractors. The appreciation of the Gospels as well-crafted works by authors with unique perspectives, alongside changing attitudes on unrecoverable sources and traditions, make Farrer's legacy important.[2]

The difficulty, in large part, was that Austin Farrer often failed to play the part of the traditional Biblical scholar.

Dennis Nineham, Farrer's successor as Warden of Keble, did not think of him as 'a professional, linguistically fully qualified, and widely recognized biblical scholar',[3] and though this judgement is somewhat unfair, Farrer's failure to engage regularly and explicitly with other scholarship contributes to the impression. As Michael Goulder notes, Farrer 'contemned the footnote',[4] and although there are smatterings of Greek in his New Testament scholarship, he rarely quotes Hebrew, and seldom discusses German scholarship.[5] At the same time, there is a playfulness in Farrer's prose that does not appeal to those less blessed than he with the ability to write with clarity and wit. F. N. Davey's lament about the reception of *A Study in St Mark* turned out to be prophetic:

> It will, however, be a pity if, put off by Dr Farrer's sometimes amusing, sometimes quite intolerable, naughtinesses, this book is not widely recognized as the most considerable and suggestive contribution to the study of St Mark's gospel that has been made for a number of years.[6]

'Paragraph-criticism'

To admirers of Farrer's work, however, his 'golden eloquence'[7] is the invitation into a more adventurous, more compelling kind of scholarship. In his day, form-criticism reigned supreme, and Farrer was not a fan. Michael Goulder summarises the difficulty:

> In 1950 Mark was widely viewed as a simple transcriber of tradition. The flood-tide of form criticism, having washed away the nineteenth-century illusion of a chronologically ordered biography of Jesus, seemed to leave the gospel paragraphs as so many independent rocks strewn by natural force along the shore. Mark as an evangelist was of little interest; he had merely taken the rocks as he had found them and linked them together in his crude style.[8]

Farrer claims to have 'no quarrel at all'[9] with form-criticism in itself. His argument is about approach and priorities. He talks disparagingly about 'paragraph-criticism' and contrasts it with looking at books as wholes:

> It is patently false that paragraph-criticism is autonomous. Paragraph-criticism and book-criticism do not even exist side by side; book-criticism must precede paragraph-criticism. No one can usefully set about paragraph-criticism until he has got the plan and purpose of the whole book into his head. Otherwise he will be in an absurd predicament, always trying to interpret features which relate principally to the whole as relating simply to the constituent part.[10]

The critique nicely anticipates what in fact began to emerge a matter of years later, *Redaktionsgeschichte*, inadequately labelled 'redaction criticism' in English-speaking scholarship,[11] which shifted the focus of Gospel analysis from the supposed building blocks of the Gospel units in oral preaching, to the crafting of the Gospels by the evangelists themselves. It was just the kind of reaction against form-criticism that Farrer had been advocating, though its pioneers seem to have been ignorant of Farrer's work, and subsequent surveys of New Testament scholarship have done little to redress the balance.

For Farrer, the way to tease out the evangelists' overarching plans was to look for signs of purpose in the arrangement of their materials. If the evangelists were not simply archivists or compilers, there must have been some kind of intelligent structuring of materials; and the possibility that there might be significant patterns sent Farrer searching for clues.

Marcan Symbolism

Not all of Farrer's suggestions about Gospel structures and symbolism are equally plausible, but the presence of more speculative suggestions should not detract from the strength of the more striking patterns. One of the best is the suggestion that Mark's healings are arranged around the number 12:

(1)   1.21–28: Demoniac
(2)   1.29–31: Simon's Mother-in-Law
(3)   1.40–45: Leper
(4)   2.1–12: Paralytic
(5)   3.1–6: Withered Hand
(6)   5.1–20: Gerasene Demoniac
(7)   5.25–34: Women with Haemorrhage
(8)   5.21–24, 35–43: Jairus' Daughter
        7.24–30: Syro-Phoenician Woman
(9)   7.31–37: Deaf Mute
(10) 8.22–26: Blind Man of Bethsaida
(11) 9.14–29: Boy with Unclean Spirit
(12) 10.46–52: Blind Bartimaeus

There are, in fact, 13 healing stories in Mark's Gospel, but Farrer suggests that 12 of them are healings of Israelites, and one of them, the Syro-Phoenician Woman (7.24–30), represents the first fruits of the Gentiles. It is, after all, this story that clearly stresses the non-Jewish nature of its heroine, her outstanding faith, and Jesus' apparent change of mind. Moreover, she is the only person in the Gospel to address Jesus as 'Lord' (Κύριε, 7.28).

Even this example is not certain, given that there are other ways that the healings could be configured. Is the Gerasene Demoniac (5.1–20), for example, also a Gentile, and should the story of Jairus' daughter and the woman with a haemorrhage (5.21–43) count as one story or two healings? The strength of the proposal, though, lies in Mark's known interest in the number 12. He frequently stresses that there are 12 disciples, even to the point of redundancy (3.16 after 3.14), and in 5.21–43, he twice mentions 'twelve years', once as the length of time of the woman's flow of blood (5.25), and once as the age of Jairus' daughter (5.42). In neither case is it necessary to the story; the narrator could simply have said 'for many years' with respect to the haemorrhaging; and he had already described Jairus' daughter as 'little daughter' (5.23) and 'little girl' (5.41). The fact that he specifically draws attention to the number 12 in both cases seems to be significant. It is the only time the narrator ever tells the reader about the length of the illness, and the only time he gives the age of the person being healed.

St Matthew and St Mark

Reviewers did not hold back on criticising Farrer's supposed patterns, and one of the concerns was his 'ingenuity and fecund imagination',[12] which in this context are cast as negatives. How could Mark have gone to so much trouble to embed subtle, skilful patterns in the Gospel only to have them ignored for almost 2,000 years? C. K. Barrett's comments are representative:

> It is somewhat surprising that the key to Mark's work, though perceived by Matthew and perhaps by Luke, should have been lost through all succeeding generations until it was recovered by Dr Farrer. Surely in antiquity, if not more recently, someone ought to have seen what Mark was about; his ingenuity seems to have been wasted.[13]

Yet there is a hint of the answer to Barrett's problem in this quotation itself. *St Matthew and St Mark*, the Edward Cadbury lectures in Birmingham (1953–4), was published only three years after *A Study in St Mark*,[14] and while it partly revises the theses of that book, it also takes them forward by attempting to develop how Mark was received by its earliest interpreter, Matthew. If Matthew could be seen to have read Mark, learned, and inwardly digested it, with hints of the same kind of patterning, this would indeed be impressive.

Unfortunately, Farrer's attempts to show that Matthew too works with a patterning around the number 12 are not as successful as his attempts to show the same in Mark, but the book nevertheless sparkles with fresh insights, and the idea of systematically thinking through Matthew as a reader and interpreter of Mark is still rewarding. 'St Matthew is St Mark's closest interpreter', Farrer says, 'and his characteristic attitude to St Mark is the desire to expound and expand. He finds his predecessor's thought too packed, too pregnant.'[15] He points out, for example, that when Mark depicts John the Baptist as Elijah: 'He was writing for men who could take up easily references which we track down painfully.'[16] Mark's hearers recognise Herod and Herodias (Mark 6.14–30) as Ahab and Jezebel, and they know that John the Baptist has been pursued by them as a new Elijah. Readers are prepared for Jesus' statement that 'Elijah has come already' (Mark 9.11–13), and the proper understanding of the identity of John the Baptist leads to a true understanding of Jesus' identity and destiny. The potential difficulty is that Mark is so allusive, so mysterious, that reading him can be puzzling to the uninitiated. For Farrer, Matthew was an intelligent, informed interpreter of Mark, who reassures his readers, lest there be any room for doubt, that John the Baptist is indeed Elijah, and that the identification is the essential pre-requisite for understanding Jesus' destiny (Matt. 17.13).[17] Matthew might be less subtle than his predecessor, but he succeeded in teasing out his source's enigmas, and Farrer is underlining it.

'On Dispensing with Q'

Although views on Farrer's Biblical scholarship vary, there is one piece for which he is justly famous, an article that has lent his name to a theory that is now far more popular than it was during his lifetime. 'On Dispensing with Q' was published in a 1955 volume edited by Dennis Nineham originally intended as a Festschrift for R. H. Lightfoot, which became a memorial volume after Lightfoot's untimely death in 1953.[18] The piece dates from the same era as *A Study in St Mark*, and *St Matthew and St Mark*, both of which flirt briefly with the question of Q,[19] the hypothetical document alleged to have been the source of 200 or so verses shared by Matthew and Luke that are not found in Mark. Farrer's article is bold but straightforward, exhilarating yet persuasive, without doubt his finest work on the New Testament. In a matter of a few pages, he attempts to overturn the ground on which the Q hypothesis stands, and he is fully aware of how daunting the task is:

> Why dig up solid foundations, why open questions long taken for settled? Much critical and expository work rests squarely on the Q hypothesis, and if the hypothesis loses credit, the nuisance will be great. The books we rely upon to guide our thought about the history of Christ will need to be read with painful and unrelaxing re-interpretation . . . Have we always to fight the old battles over again? Minds of high ability and scrupulous integrity were brought to bear on the Q question in the great days of source-criticism. They sifted to the bottom, they counted every syllable, and they agreed in the substance of their findings. Is it likely that we, whose attention is distracted by the questions of our day, can profitably do their work again? And what reason have we to trust our judgement against theirs, if we find ourselves dissenting from their conclusions?[20]

The fundamental insight is clear. It is an application of Occam's Razor, an insistence that since good sense can be made of Luke's use of Matthew, their non-Marcan agreements do not require the postulation of an extra, hypothetical document:[21]

> [T]he Q hypothesis . . . wholly depends on the incredibility of St Luke's having read St Matthew's book. That incredibility depends in turn on the supposition that St Luke was essentially an adapter and compiler. We do not now, or ought not now, so to regard him. And being once rid of such a supposition, we can conceive well enough how St Luke could have both read St Matthew's book as it stands, and written the gospel he has left us.[22]

Farrer's arguments were both offensive and defensive, positively arguing for Luke's use of Matthew, while answering Streeter's highly influential arguments against the view.[23] Streeter had argued that Luke could not have used Matthew given the dramatically different placement of the non-Marcan material they shared, but Farrer points out that one needs to make sense of Luke's Gospel on its own terms:

> We are not bound to show that what St Luke did to St Matthew turned out to be a literary improvement on St Matthew. All we have to show is that St Luke's plan was capable of attracting St Luke. You do not like what I have done to the garden my predecessor left me. You are welcome to your opinion, but I did what I did because I thought I should prefer the new arrangement. And if you want to enjoy whatever special merit my gardening has, you must forget my predecessor's ideas and try to appreciate mine.[24]

With similar elegance, Farrer disposes of other specious arguments against Luke's use of Matthew. Where advocates of Q point to the 'more primitive appearance' of Luke's versions of sayings he shares with Matthew, Farrer notes the subjectivity of the judgements being made. 'There is scarcely an instance in which we can determine priority of form without invoking questionable assumptions.'[25] Where scholars point to Luke's omission of Matthean materials, Farrer points out that one would only expect Luke to take over material pleasing to him, and that the Q material is characterised in just this way – it appears to be 'those parts of St Matthew's non-Marcan material which were likely to attract St Luke'.[26]

One of the strengths of Farrer's article is that unlike less successful challenges to the dominant Two-Source Theory, he presupposes and builds on the shared element of Marcan Priority. He draws attention to ways in which Matthew and Luke appear to converge in their editing of Mark. Minor agreements between the two keep appearing. 'Now this is just what one would expect', Farrer says, 'on the supposition that St Luke had read St Matthew, but decided to work direct upon the more ancient narrative of St Mark for himself. He does his own work of adaptation, but small Matthaean echoes keep appearing, because St Luke is after all acquainted with St Matthew.'[27]

The article, while brilliant, is not perfect. Farrer could not resist an unnecessary, speculative exposition of how Luke rewrote Matthew's 'Pentateuch', producing in his central section a kind of 'Christian Deuteronomy',[28] lending the impression that dispensing with Q involves problematic commitment to the kind of patterning that Farrer loved but his critics often disliked. It is not surprising that Stephen Neill concluded: 'I think that Q has come to stay.'[29] And for those unfamiliar with the joys of Farrer's prose, his rhetoric can come off as idiosyncrasy, even ignorance. One typical Farrer flourish, focusing on the hypothetical nature of Q, has proved an easy target:

> The Q hypothesis is a hypothesis, that is its weakness. To be rid of it we have no need of a contrary hypothesis, we merely have to make St Luke's use of St Matthew intelligible; and to understand what St Luke made of St Matthew we need no more than to consider what St Luke made of his own book. Now St Luke's book is not a hypothetical entity. Here is a copy of it on my desk . . .[30]

The copy of Luke's Gospel on Farrer's desk in Trinity College was not, of course, identical with the evangelist's autograph, and critics were quick to point out that scholarly reconstructions of the New Testament texts are themselves, in a sense, 'hypothetical'.[31] But to overinterpret the rhetoric misses the point of Farrer's contrast, which is between a theory that solves the Synoptic Problem by invoking an additional, non-extant work, and one that does not.

Farrer's article, then, did not cause Q to collapse. The impertinence, for some, was simply too great. R. H. Fuller wrote in 1962 that 'It is hard to think that the patient work over many years . . . can be blithely dismissed in a few pages',[32] and he was right. The case against Q required a great deal more. For Farrer's student

Michael Goulder, who took on the mantle,[33] 'It was a vision, but the vision is for many days'.[34] Strong ideas can pick up momentum when the pioneer's students, and their students' students, take an interest. They move to maturity as the wider scholarly world begins to take an interest. Fifty years after Farrer's death, he is as well known for 'the Farrer theory' of Synoptic origins, now a major competitor in the field, as he is for anything else.[35]

The Final Manuscript

For Farrer, scholarship was always in progress, and he was never reluctant to rethink his own ideas. 'Our life is a continual repentance', he said; 'and if we are so rash as to publish our opinions, that repentance will be in part a public one.'[36] It is sadly fitting that when he died so unexpectedly in 1968, he was in the middle of a manuscript on Mark's Gospel that continued the process of refining and developing the ideas found in *A Study in St Mark* and *St Matthew and St Mark*. With the exception of the first eight pages,[37] the unfinished manuscript, which has the title 'St Mark's Material' in Farrer's hand at the top of the first page, has never seen the light of day.[38] The manuscript is 80 or so yellowing manuscript pages, some of it in typescript but most of it in Farrer's fountain pen. Several of the pages are recycled, including ballots of a Keble College bursarial committee and tutorial committee with the note, 'Please return to the Warden by Saturday, 22 June', which shows that Farrer was writing the manuscript in the second half of 1968, a fact confirmed by two of his undergraduate students at the time, John Muddiman, and John Barton, who had extra tutorials to discuss the developing project.[39]

The manuscript is unmistakably Farrer, with several of his keynote ideas, now developing in fresh ways. He is still thinking hard about how to read Mark in the light of 'Old Testament models', including a lengthy excursus on 'Levi the Son of Alphaeus' in which he suggests looking again at the 12 disciples against the backdrop of the 12 tribes, and he frequently breaks up the text to illustrate the patterns he is finding in diagram form. In spite of the heading, 'St Mark's Material',

Farrer is still focused throughout the manuscript on attempting to explore Mark's mind, and to understand his method. He pursues the author by understanding his finished work:

> We must first settle this question, what an author as a matter of historical fact intended to say. For a written book is simply the expression of a writer's mind; to understand the text is to understand the author: not the author outside the book, but the author as author of the book. It is peculiar to legal documents that they should be allowed to bear whatever sense logically be placed upon the words composing them. We do not read a book – you do not, I trust, read mine – to discover what it can be fairly made to mean; we read it to perceive what its author does or did mean.[40]

This focus on the author brings with it Farrer's now familiar disdain for form-criticism. He repeatedly expresses his dissatisfaction with the status quo of 1960s Gospel scholarship:

> How do we show what must be 'editorial'? Here is St Mark at work – you can read his book and see what belongs to the continuous progress of his thoughts – if that is what you mean by detecting the editorial element. But somewhat to our amazement we find another method commonly preferred. You start from the other end, with the invisible and unknown. You conjecture the form which the tradition must have taken in those pre-Marcan decades. It must, you think, have consisted of short, mutually independent, anecdotes or dicta; it must have dealt with a certain range of topics; and so on.[41]

Farrer suggests that even where Mark's materials might appear to conform to 'oral tradition' archetypes, this is because of Mark's own moulding of the material in an oral environment that was familiar with the Elijah-Elisha stories, and other Scriptural precedents.

Overall, the manuscript is sadly more rough than ready, and if it is ironic that, like Mark's Gospel itself, it is unfinished,[42] it seems strangely appropriate that like Farrer's Biblical scholarship overall, it was a work in progress.

Farrer's Legacy

In the conclusion to 'On Dispensing with Q', Farrer begins to look to the future of Biblical scholarship. 'Let us indulge ourselves a little here, and prophesy', he says, continuing:

> The literary history of the Gospels will turn out to be a simpler matter than we had supposed. St Matthew will be seen to be an amplified version of St Mark, based on a decade of habitual preaching, and incorporating oral material, but presupposing no other literary source beside St Mark himself. St Luke, in turn, will be found to presuppose St Matthew and St Mark, and St John to presuppose the three others. The whole literary history of the canonical Gospel tradition will be found to be contained in the fourfold canon itself, except in so far as it lies in the Old Testament, the Pseudepigrapha, and the other New Testament writings.[43]

If there is an elegance about Farrer's vision for the future of New Testament scholarship, there is also some economy. While many today would baulk at Farrer's 'canonical bias', and his almost complete lack of interest in materials that lie outside of the Christian Bible, that very focus disciplined his mind to explore all kinds of possible links between the Scriptures that inspired him, the Scriptures that he saw as inspiring one another. Every piece of Scriptural interpretation is a story of inspiration from other Scriptures. Farrer scarcely utters a word on Mark without thinking about Old Testament types and patterns; Matthew is Mark's first and most important interpreter, just as Luke's work only makes sense if the evangelist is reworking his predecessors' Gospels; and 'St John is careful to respect the Marcan outline, even though he writes all round it rather than inside it'.[44] Farrer was a source-critical minimalist, but the canonical constraints that he set himself drew important lines between early Christian works, lines that many could not see. The by-product of his per-spective was that he could put form-criticism in its place, and dispense with Q, while both were enjoying their ascendancy. He did not live to see the growing movement against the Q hypoth-esis, and redaction criticism was only in its infancy when he died,[45] but in these respects at least, he does seem prophetic.[46]

It would be a mistake, though, to dwell on Farrer's pre-science at the expense of remembering his historical context. His scholarship will seem old-fashioned to many today, with its sermonic undertones, its lack of footnotes, its focus on inspiration, and its talk about 'St Mark' and 'St Matthew' and how they and the other evangelists were 'moved'. Yet to appre-ciate Farrer's Biblical scholarship is to understand its ground-ing in his theology. Inspiration, for Farrer, is observable, and the Spirit's moving is discerned in the pages of Gospels. It is tempting to say that Farrer's mode for thinking about how the evangelists worked bears a marked similarity to his own mind, with symbols giving birth to patterns in poetic prose. When dwelling on Mark's mind, Farrer writes:

> He feels in his bones the power of one historical phase to beget the next because, as he writes, he experiences the power of one cycle of narrative to beget its own exposition of development in the next cycle. What the Spirit of his inspi-ration does with his thoughts is but the tracing over of what Creative Power did with the events about which he thinks.[47]

Tracing inspiration is the Biblical theologian's task. To investigate Scripture is to interpret the divine.

Notes

1 Anonymous, 1968.

2 This article focuses on Farrer's Gospel scholarship, but it is important to bear in mind also his contribution to the study of the Apocalypse, Farrer, 1949 and Farrer, 1964a. For studies of Farrer's Biblical scholarship, see in particular Titley, 2010.

3 Nineham, 1994, p. xiii. In context, Nineham is praising Goulder, Farrer's student, while disparaging his teacher.

4 Goulder, 1985, p. 193.

5 Even here, though, Farrer's 'An English Appreciation' of Bultmann's work (Farrer, 1961) ranks among his most compelling writing.

6 Davey, 1952. Cf. Jeffrey Peterson, 'Austin Farrer's Marcan Criticism', unpublished paper presented to Southwest Biblical Seminar, Dallas, Texas, 15 October 2004, shared with permission: 'I suspect further that Farrer's lyrical, sometimes whimsical prose did not commend his work to NT students, as on paper we are by and large a humorless lot, formulating hypotheses and weighing evidence in the grave manner learned from our Teutonic masters, and the presumption is widespread among us that profit and delight are mutually exclusive.'

7 Goulder, 1985, p. 201.

8 Goulder, 1985, p. 205.

9 Farrer, 1951, p. 21.

10 Farrer, 1951, p. 23.

11 For an introduction and comment, see Goodacre, 2008b.

12 Barrett, 1956, p. 109.

13 Barrett, 1956, pp. 109–10.

14 Farrer, 1954.

15 Farrer, 1954, p. 4.

16 Farrer, 1954, p. 5.

17 For an attempt at developing Farrer's insight, see Goodacre, 2008a.

18 Farrer, 1955.

19 Note in particular Farrer, 1951, p. 210: 'But when you try to define its existence in itself by where, when, and what, you fall into contradictions.'

20 Farrer, 1955, p. 55.

21 Although there is no evidence that Farrer had read them, there are important precedents for the theory of Marcan Priority alongside Luke's familiarity with Matthew, including Lummis, 1925–6, and Ropes, 1934, 1960.

22 Farrer, 1955, p. 56.

23 Streeter, 1924.

24 Farrer, 1955, p. 65.

25 Farrer, 1955, p. 64.

26 Farrer, 1955, p. 57.

27 Farrer, 1955, p. 61. For a fuller discussion of the major and minor agreements, see Goodacre, 2002, chapter 8.

28 Farrer, 1955, pp. 73–82.

29 Neill and Wright, 1988, p. 136 n. 1.

30 Farrer, 1955, p. 66.

31 See, for example, Kloppenborg, 2003, pp. 214–15 n. 13; and Kloppenborg, 2014, 'a sleight of hand' (p. 48).

32 Fuller, 1963, p. 74 n. 1.

33 Michael Goulder developed Farrer's theory in several publications, the most important of which is Goulder, 1989. Some scholars use the term 'Farrer-Goulder theory' to honour Goulder's key contribution.

34 Goulder, 1985, p. 197.

35 See most recently Poirier and Peterson, 2015; Nielsen and Müller, 2016.

36 Farrer, 1954, p. 1.

37 These were published posthumously in Farrer, 1976c, pp. 14–22.

38 The manuscript was in the possession of Michael Goulder until his death in 2010. I am currently transcribing and editing the manuscript with a view to publication.

39 I am grateful to John Barton for this information.

40 Farrer, Unpublished Manuscript, i.

41 Farrer, Unpublished Manuscript, vi.

42 It is worth noting, however, that Farrer presciently anticipated those who saw 16.8 as a fitting conclusion to Mark's Gospel, 'The mere rustling of the hem of his risen glory, the voice of the boy in the white robe, turns them to headlong flight: "and they said not a word to anyone, for they were afraid". Do we stop there or do we go on? I think we stop' (Farrer, 1948, p. 140).

43 Farrer, 1955, p. 85.

44 Farrer, 1951, p. 211. His treatment of John in relation to Mark is on pp. 210–20.

45 Cf. Neill and Wright, 1988, pp. 282–3, which lauds Farrer for his insights against form-criticism, while noting the simultaneous emergence of the German school of *Redaktionsgeschichte*.

46 See also Peterson, 2000, which argues that Farrer also anticipated the perspectives of narrative critics.

47 Farrer, 1951, p. xx.

Farrer on the Problem of Evil

MICHAEL F. LLOYD

I have given my academic life to the Problem of Evil, and Austin Farrer's *Love Almighty and Ills Unlimited* remains the best-written book on the Problem of Evil I have yet read. When it came out, the *Church Times* described it as having 'a scintillating style'[1] and, to show you that that is not an overstatement, let me begin with a rather delightful snippet.

Farrer imagines a philosophical discussion with his gardening neighbour:

> While I am prosing away in this strain, and riding my philosophical hobby, my gardening neighbour takes up his fork, and returns to the attack on his old enemy, the ground elder. With a sudden grunt, he rears up, and lays his hand on his loins. 'Lumbago,' he says. 'And what about that? Are you going to say that it's good in itself and only bad for me? Or that it's bad in itself by failing to be a really good pain? It's quite good enough at being a pain, if you ask me. I should say it's a thoroughly bad thing.'
>
> 'Thoroughly bad,' I reply, 'but not a thing. On the packet of Dr Sidebottom's Lumbago Powder, the disease is represented as a somewhat scraggy little dragon, biting a sufferer in the part affected; while Dr Sidebottom (if he is the figure with the high collar and the luxuriant moustaches) pitches into the aggressor with an outsize toasting fork . . . But your lumbago is not a dragon – it is only you, or a bit of you, misfunctioning and hurting. To call it bad is to say that it would be good for you neither to hurt nor to misfunction

in this way, but to enjoy what you optimistically call your usual health.'

My friend, defeated by lumbago if not by argument, abandons the garden, and the discussion. I go my own way, convinced, as usual, by my own voice.[2]

A scintillating style makes a book more enjoyable, but it does not make an argument more compelling. What is Farrer's argument?

Farrer's Theodicy

I have argued elsewhere[3] that Christian responses to the Problem of Evil may be classified under three categories: 1) Evil as Inimical to the purposes of God, 2) Evil as Instrumental to the purposes of God, 3) Evil as Inevitable within the purposes of God.

The view of Evil as *inimical* to the purposes of God points to the healing and nature miracles of Jesus and sees in them the divine attitude towards sickness, suffering and threat – which it sees as hostility. It therefore refuses to allow that suffering and threat have any divinely legitimated place within cosmic processes, or cosmic history, or human history. Hence it has to tell a narrative about how creation came to be at odds with the purposes of its Creator – in other words, it has to posit some sort of cosmic fall.

Farrer allows that

since sin is voluntary, it need never, ideally speaking, have been committed; men could have gone right from the start . . . we do not know what damage original sin has done us, because we do not know what the position of mankind would now be, if no one had sinned.[4]

But 'we can talk rationally enough about the ravages of sin; what strife and cruelty, lust, pride, sloth, and indifference have done'.[5]

The supreme misfortune is sin itself; a perverse attitude to God, our neighbour, and our own claims or concerns. But how many other mental ills does it bring in its train! The material anxieties, the personal mortifications, the stings of unsatisfied ambition or of vain remorse . . . And death itself – sin did not literally introduce it, but how much sin has embittered the sting![6]

So much he allows. What he does *not* allow is that sin has made human beings mortal, or vulnerable to injury or disease. In other words, he sees sin as the cause of *moral* evil, but refuses to see sin as the cause of *natural* evil: 'Sin may have built the slums, it did not breed the bacilli. It has made many wars, perhaps all; but droughts and earthquakes, no.'[7] So Farrer does not deny that suffering is inimical to the purposes of God – he does describe the death of a child as not only 'a wound in the body of human affection', but also 'an undoubted flaw in the order of nature'[8] – but it is not where the weight of his theodicy lies.

So let us turn to the view of Evil as *instrumental* to the purposes of God. That's the view that suffering is deliberately built in to creation, that it is planned by God as God's instrument to work his purposes in us – to mature us, to deepen us, to give us opportunities for courage (which is not possible without threat), or for compassion (which is not possible without suffering). Farrer allows for this possibility in passing – 'Sufferings nobly endured may be the gymnastic of the soul'[9] – but he is highly reluctant to go far in this direction, because he is all too aware that suffering may embitter rather than ennoble, destroy rather than deepen. Panglossian spouters of popular wisdom

like to say that what happened was all for the best. They are probably wrong. Good . . . is a more fertile breeder of good on the whole . . . than distress of any kind can be. Were it otherwise, we should be faced with an intolerable dilemma. We should be bound to fear that in consulting our friends' natural happiness, we should be imperilling their spiritual salvation . . . Good breeds more good than any evil can.[10]

He gives the instrumental view of evil even shorter shrift than the inimical view of evil.

No, where the weight of Farrer's theodicy lies is in the view of evil as *inevitable* within the purposes of God.[11]

> Poor, limping world, why does not your kind Creator pull the thorn out of your paw? But what sort of a thorn is this? And if it were pulled out, how much of the paw would remain? How much, indeed, of the creation? What would a physical universe be like, from which all mutual interference of systems was eliminated? It would be no physical universe at all. It would not be like an animal relieved of pain by the extraction of a thorn. It would be like an animal rendered incapable of pain by the removal of its nervous system; that is to say, of its animality. So the physical universe could be delivered from the mutual interference of its constituent systems, only by being deprived of its physicality.[12]

Farrer admits that 'in the many and various interactions of the world, there are innumerable misfits, vast damage to systems, huge destruction and waste',[13] and he asks, 'Why is it so, if God is wise and almighty?' He replies first by questioning whether a more smoothly fitting world would be preferable, and then by questioning whether it would be possible. He answers both in the negative. It would not be preferable because

> Gone will be that enormous vitality of force, which makes every system or concentration of energy to radiate over the whole field of space, every living kind to propagate without restraint, and, in a word, every physical creature to absolutize itself, so far as in it lies, and to be the whole world, if it can. It cannot, admittedly; and why? Because of interference from a million rivals, all equally reckless in their own vitality. Eliminate the mutual interferences, and gone, equally, will be the drama of an existence continually at stake, of a being which has to be achieved and held, of the unexpected

and the improvised[14] . . . It is impossible to see how strife between them [different life forms] is to be avoided, if they are to run their own world in this active fashion.[15]

And a smoothly fitting physical world would not, in any case, be possible because 'only pure spirits could be wholly non-destructive'.[16]

Why, then, did God not make a spiritual rather than a physical world? If all physical beings are bound to be seeking to absolutise themselves and thereby to be in conflict with one another, then why did God not limit his creation to pure spirits who alone could be relied upon to be wholly non-destructive? Answer: because spiritual beings would be too close to their Creator to be able to be free, or, indeed, to be anything at all. 'The divine glory would draw them into itself, as the candle draws the moth.'[17] So there needed to be some sort of a screen between God and his creatures, to shield them from the otherwise irresistible lure of their Creator. Physicality is that screen.

So Farrer's fundamental theodicy is that you can't have a physical world without a destructive clash of the systems. And you can't have individuality and freedom without physicality. Hence the inevitability of evil within the purposes of God.

Given that God has to set up the creation in this way, why does he not intervene within it more often, in order to relieve animal suffering? After all, *we* would!

The question is not unamiable, but it is confused. God loves his animal creatures by being God to them . . . not by being a brother creature to them, as he does for mankind in the unique miracle of his incarnation. He provides them with brother-saviours, or sometimes human saviours, through the working of compassion, and not otherwise.[18]

And the final building block of his theodicy is his eschatology:

Though modern Christians may disown a literal belief in any . . . wonder due to appear on a calendar day, or to fill a visible sky, they will be ill-advised to let go the substance of an expectation which can alone make luminous to them the purposes of God.[19]

How may we evaluate this theodicy? There is much to welcome.

An Evaluation of Farrer's Theodicy: the Positives

First, we may, I suggest, welcome the fact that he so decisively rejects the view of evil as instrumental to the purposes of God. This is partly for the pastoral reason that he gives (namely that suffering as often destroys as deepens), and partly for the Christological reason that what we see in the person of Christ is a divine assault on suffering – not a divine education of humanity as to the benefits to be found within it. As the Cornish poet Jack Clemo points out: 'When the storm arose on Gennesaret he did not bid the disciples to humble themselves devoutly before the "great Being" who was trying to drown them . . .' (Nor, we might add, did he bid them be educated by the extremity of their experience, nor pay heed to the voice of God shouting to them through the megaphone of pain, nor exult in the drama of an existence continually – and, right now, especially – at stake.) No, 'He lashed back at the elements from his bridgehead in the divine kingdom.'[20] In the Matthean narrative, he did not invite the man with leprosy to look for the hand of God in his experience of decomposition and exclusion: the hand of God was to be seen in Jesus' own hand, stretched out to heal.[21] In the Marcan narrative, he did not invite the paralysed man to reflect on the compassion he had induced in his friends: he told him to take up his mat and walk.[22] In the Lucan narrative, he did not tell the mourners in Jairus' house to stop wailing because death is nothing at all or because it is part of the purposes of God – but because of his power to undo it.[23] In the Johannine narrative, he faced the death of Lazarus, not with resignation and equanimity, but with grief and anger – and with action that reversed the wrong of

Lazarus' death.[24] The New Testament presents suffering and death not as intentionally implanted into the creation by the Creator as his inexplicable instruments, but as assaulted in the ministry of Jesus and finally to be undone when the first things have passed away.[25]

Second, his assertion that 'God loves his animal creatures by being God to them' seems to me to be an original and helpful contribution to theodicy. The frequently made contention that God, by omitting to perform acts of suffering-prevention that a moderately moral human being would perform, demonstrates thereby either his non-goodness, or his non-existence, fails to take into account the seriousness and irrevocability of human vice-regency. We are called to rule,[26] and God, unlike a driving instructor, does not operate a dual control, whereby he may wrest that rule back from us whenever we deviate from his purposes. Redemption does not take back that delegated rule – it restores it.[27] The statement often (and probably wrongly) attributed to St Theresa of Avila, that 'Christ has no body on earth now but yours, no hands but yours, no feet but yours' is *physically speaking* correct. Witness the difficulty in thinking of any reportedly divine act in Scripture which is not mediated in some way by creaturely agency. The atheologian's argument that God's neglect of acts of suffering-prevention which we would not neglect counts against his existence fails, therefore, to give sufficient weight to the decisiveness of the Ascension, too. God's restriction of himself to *divine* activity and his refusal to stand in for and supplant *human* activity arguably strengthens the significance, the seriousness and the necessity of our moral action.

Third, the insistence of the theodical necessity of a strong eschatology (at a time when it was being underplayed in much contemporary theology, both academic and popular-level) was then – and is always – a timely reminder. As Farrer put it:

Anyone can spin phrases about a world hidden from sight, where all journeys end, and from which no traveller returns. And yet there is no other consolation but this which carries any force. The issue is all or nothing; either we believe, or we do not . . . Has the boy perished as though he had never been, and is his father to go the same way in a few years? Then how trivial it is that the old man should sublimate his disappointed parenthood in an enthusiasm for the reclamation of young gangsters! He has begun his charitable work somewhat late in life; it is not to be thought that he will make much of a showing at it. But once admit that the characters of the tragedy are immortal souls, and the balance alters. The boy's premature death, though an undoubted flaw in the order of nature, and a wound in the body of human affection, is not so blank a loss as to make the mention of redeeming consequences an indecency; while the opening of the father's narrow heart, being the preparation of a soul for glory and a beginning of heaven on earth, obtains a weight which may fairly tell in the scale of compensations. Even the old man's ill-practised philanthropy begins to have an incalculable radiation. He may not appear an effective agent in his chosen work, but divine charity once lighted in him will kindle his fellow-workers, or awake a response somewhere. And all charity, visible or invisible to human eyes, is everlasting life.[28]

Farrer is right, I suggest, in his assertion of the importance of eschatology *as consolation*. If it is relationship that makes life worthwhile, then death haemorrhages that worthwhileness, and only the hope of those deep relationships being restored can re-establish that worthwhileness. As Nicholas Wolterstorff wrote about the death of his son in a climbing accident: 'For that grief, what consolation can there be other than having him back?'[29]

Farrer is right, too, I believe, in noticing the importance of eschatology *for meaning*. Without an eschatological hope, a late change of heart and life does little to alter the overall impact of a person's life: with such a hope, it has an eternal forward trajectory and an incalculable outward radiation.

But eschatology is also vital *for the whole project of theodicy*. For, just as one does not know the meaning of a novel until one has read to the end, so the meaning – and, indeed, the worthwhileness – of creation only reveals itself in the light of the end. Just as 'nobody knows who I am till the judgement morning',[30] so nobody can understand the cosmos – nor evaluate the decision of the Creator to create – except in the light of eschatology. Eschatological hope in no way justifies or lessens the evil of suffering, but it may help justify the decision to create, despite the horrors of suffering that would stain cosmic history.

His rejection of the instrumental view of evil, his assertion that God acts in his world *as God*, and his insistence on the importance of eschatology for theodicy seem to me to be significant contributions to theodical discussion – of which the second is the most original.

On the other hand, there are also some significant challenges to Farrer's theodicy.

An Evaluation of Farrer's Theodicy: the Challenges

As we noted above, Farrer argues that a more smoothly fitting world would be undesirable and impossible. We shall consider these two claims in turn.

Would a more smoothly fitting world be undesirable?

His argument that a world without the mutual interference of systems would be undesirable is highly questionable. His eloquent praise of 'that enormous vitality of force' which makes 'every physical creature to absolutize itself, so far as in it lies, and to be the whole world' seems quasi-Nietzschean in its endorsement of the will to power.[31]

Farrer asks: 'if the several systems are to occupy just as much free space each as they need, without crowding their neighbours; if none is ever to incorporate any part of another in itself, except in such fashion that it preserves or even enhances the self-being of that other; then what sort of a world shall we have?'[32] The answer would seem to be: one that reflects the kenotic, self-sacrificing nature of a God who, as Rowan Williams likes to say, 'does not compete with us for space'.[33] The answer would seem to be 'one which reflects the God revealed on the cross, who is more concerned for the flourishing of others than of Himself'.

If a Trinitarian conception of God models a non-competitive inter-relationship in which each person is fully themselves in a way that contributes to (and in no way threatens) the identity, glory and beatific bliss of the others, would we not expect a world created by that Trinity to reflect those divine interactions by (at the very least) the non-destructiveness of its several parts? And is not the incompatibility of mutual destructiveness with the righteousness and wisdom of God precisely the insight embodied in the prophetic vision of the wolf lying down with the lamb? Is it not the implication of our Trinitarianly grounded belief in what John Milbank calls 'the ontological priority of peace over conflict'[34] that, in the creation of the God of peace, no element in that creation would harm or destroy any other element[35] (unless there had been an hiatic and creaturely caused deviation from the purposes of the Creator)?

Why should a Christian theodicy adopt a definition of vitality which looks worryingly like the will to power? And why should a harmonious set of interactions, reflecting the inner life of the Trinity, be denigrated as being limp, undramatic, and lacking in energy, challenge, novelty and surprise? Yet that would seem to be the implication behind Farrer's value judgement here. There seems to be an almost pagan exalting in the challenge of one life pitted against another, and in the vitality of perpetual conflict. Whereas, I suggest that the cross reveals a much different paradigm. Through the cross God proves himself to be the One who lays down his life that others might live. In stark contrast with the natural world in which animals kill others so that they themselves might live, God's movement of self-giving is in the opposite direction from that of ruthless self-preservation.[36]

Should those who worship a crucified God, therefore, celebrate the human urge to absolutise oneself at the expense of the other? This human will to power runs contrary to the nature of a God who did not set out to be the world but created a world that is both contingent and not-God. He revealed himself in the self-giving example of Jesus Christ, who, rather than absolutising himself, made himself nothing and took the very nature of a servant; who, rather than pushing aside the weak or exerting himself upon them, gave them dignity by asking them 'what would you have me do for you?' Most significantly, the will to power is antithetical to the self-emptying pattern of Jesus, who, far from killing others to preserve his own life, gave up his own life that others might live. In his humiliation and exaltation, the crucified God 'incorporated creaturehood into Himself precisely in order to preserve and enhance the self-being of that creation'.[37]

So, if a more smoothly fitting world would, *pace* Farrer, be more desirable, is he right in thinking it impossible?

Would a more smoothly fitting world be impossible?

Farrer argues that it would. His argument for this position has two stages. First, he insists that a physical world is necessarily a world of mutual interference and mutual destruction: 'Our stomachs ruthlessly destroy what they consume, and if we spare animals, we shall still butcher vegetables.'[38] However, this is an assertion, rather than an argument. Furthermore, the use of the word 'butcher' surreptitiously endows vegetables with the same sort of life and value as animals. It is possible to envisage a viable physical world in which animals consume vegetables in such a way that the organism is not harmed. The eating of sprouts does not necessarily kill the plant which bears them. It is not therefore inconceivable that a physical world might operate on the basis of a form of consumption that is not ethically objectionable. Much more work would need to be done to justify Farrer's assertion that a more smoothly fitting physical world would not be possible.

Having asserted that physical beings could not be non-destructive, Farrer goes on to say that 'Only pure spirits could be wholly non-destructive', and this raises the question as to whether the Creator should have created a world of purely spiritual beings. This he rejects, on the basis that, if creatures were created to live, move and have their being in the full vision of God, it would be impossible for them to turn away from God, and they would thus not have significant freedom. They would be drawn to God like a moth to a candle. In order to preserve their freedom, therefore, it is necessary to place some sort of a screen between them and God. Arguing that a spiritual screen is incoherent, Farrer suggests that only a physical screen – or, rather, the screen that is physicality – will serve the purpose of preserving the freedom of the creature. Thus a purely spiritual world is not possible. So his total argument is that a physical world is necessarily characterised by mutual destructiveness, and a purely spiritual world is not possible. Hence, God, desiring to create, had to create something like the sort of world in which we live. A more smoothly fitting world than ours is not a possibility.

This assertion/assumption has been attacked by a number of writers, on a variety of grounds. We shall examine four: logical, theological, exegetical and doxological.

Objection on Logical Grounds

Keith Ward argues on logical grounds against the assumption that it would be impossible to be free in the immediate presence of the Creator. Ward sees this position as taking refuge within 'the Platonic dictum that to have knowledge of the Good is necessarily to *be* good: to know God is to trust Him'. Yet, Ward argues, 'one could never be said to "reject" God on this view: one could only be said to reject that of which one is aware; but man chooses the world only because he is not fully aware of God. His choice arises purely through ignorance . . .'[39] For, to be free, 'the moral agent must be fully conscious of what is being rejected as well as of what is being accepted . . . Far from "epistemic distance" from God being a condition of choice, it would constitute an unfair limitation of the agent's knowledge of the alternatives open to him, and would thus restrict his choice.' He therefore concludes that

> there is . . . no absurdity in the notion of a creature, existing in full consciousness of its Creator and yet free to reject the Creator's love for and demand upon its existence. There is no absurdity in the idea of its seeing rebellion as a possibility, for the simple reason that rebellion is a possibility within the providence of God, and a possibility the existence of which is a condition of moral freedom.[40]

Objection on Theological Grounds

Farrer's concept of physicality as a screen is close to John Hick's idea of physicality providing necessary epistemic distance from God, Jürgen Moltmann's use of the Kabbalistic notion of *zimzum*, and John Polkinghorne's metaphor of physicality as a veil. The common thread in each of these concepts is that God's overt presence would make the freedom of creatures impossible:[41] God would therefore need to absent himself from his handiwork to permit any meaningful freedom in creation. Polkinghorne writes, 'The present creation exists at some distance from its creator. Of course, God is present to this world, but in a way that is veiled, so that creatures are not overwhelmed by the sheer power and majesty of divine reality.'[42] Does this not imply, however, that space is a zero-sum game between God and creation, such that the presence of God necessarily threatens human freedom? Is it not a (pagan) misconception to assert that God's presence impinges upon creaturely freedom? Is there any place where creatures are more fully themselves and experience more freedom than in the direct presence of God? Moreover, does not such a construction presuppose that God himself is a spatial being, part of his own creation? Moltmann's claim that God's withdrawal into himself would allow 'creation the space for its own being'[43] must ultimately be rejected on the grounds that, as Williams puts it (see above), 'God does not compete with us for space'.[44]

Objection on Exegetical Grounds

According to much recent scholarship, biblical eschatology presents a universe that is smoothly fitting and not less than physical as the divinely intended destination of the cosmos. It gives us an eschatological anthropology in which it is the resurrection of the body rather than the immortality of the soul that is the divinely intended destination of the human person.[45] It gives us an eschatological cosmology in which a new *earth* is promised as well as a new heavens.[46] And it gives us an eschatological ecology that promises a coming reconciliation of predator and prey, in accordance with the prophetic vision.[47]

By contrast, Farrer has largely to Platonise his eschatology, in order to maintain his precept of the inevitability of destructive accident within a physical universe, because any harmony can only come about in the spiritual realm: '. . . it is our universal faith', he says, 'that he [God] will immortalize ourselves, in such a way that we shall cease to be physical in the ordinary sense'.[48] A lot will depend, of course, on what content is given to the phrase 'in the ordinary sense'. However, he seems also to suggest that Christ himself will not be able to be visible in glory except in and through his saints: 'What else in fact is the visible glory of Christ, but the company of his redeemed?'[49] This seems to be close to a denial of the physicality of Jesus' resurrection.[50]

If the only way to preserve Farrer's theodical assertion (that a smoothly fitting physical world is impossible) is by sailing Christologically close to the Docetic wind, anthropologically close to the Gnostic wind, and eschatologically close to the Platonic wind, then those who read the New Testament as being more committed to physicality will begin to question the assertion.

Objection on Doxological Grounds

In Chapter 3 of John Steinbeck's novel *Of Mice and Men*, there is a remarkable episode in which George tells the rather simple Lennie to jump in the river, knowing he can't swim. He watches him thrash about for a while, and then helps him out. And Lennie is pathetically grateful to George for rescuing him – apparently forgetting that it was George who was responsible for him being in the river in the first place.

It is one of the privileges of the Church that 'you may declare the praises of Him who called you out of darkness into His wonderful light'.[51] It somewhat detracts from those praises if it was God who placed us in that darkness in the first place. Could we muster whole-hearted praise for a God who rescues us from a situation he had deliberately created from the outset? Austin Farrer speaks of God as 'our rescuer from that whirlpool, in which all things, whether good or evil, senseless or sentient, are sucked down'.[52] Yet if he created that whirlpool and placed us within it, how fulsome will be our praise? How does it differ from George helping Lennie out of the river?

Conclusion

This chapter has examined Farrer's theodical position, and subjected that position to an evaluation, finding that it makes a major contribution to the field, but also faces significant challenges. Farrer's major contribution is that, while rejecting the instrumental view of evil, he situates it within an eschatological horizon in which God's loving posture towards creation in the present age always acts *as God* rather than supplanting human activity. While Farrer's contribution is to be praised, his theodicy still falls short by denying the desirability or even the possibility of a more smoothly fitting world in which God's presence does not threaten creaturely freedom – a denial that constrains the sort of eschatology he is able to offer.

I have elsewhere argued more thoroughly for my rejection of the theodicy that views evil as inevitable within the purposes of

God. I have contended, rather, that evil is inimical to the purposes of God.[53] Now, like Farrer himself, 'I go my own way, convinced, as usual, by my own voice' – but not so naïve as to imagine that my readers will be!

Notes

1 Quoted on the back cover of the 1966 Fontana edition of *Love Almighty and Ills Unlimited*.
2 Farrer, 1966, pp. 29–30 (first published Farrer, 1962).
3 Lloyd, 2018b.
4 Farrer, 1966, pp. 151, 154.
5 Farrer, 1966, p. 155.
6 Farrer, 1966, pp. 156–7.
7 Farrer, 1966, p. 159.
8 Farrer, 1966, p. 169.
9 Farrer, 1966, p. 111.
10 Farrer, 1966, pp. 167–8.
11 For a recent exposition of the 'Evil as Inevitable' view, see Southgate, 2008.
12 Farrer, 1966, p. 51.
13 Farrer, 1966, p. 52.
14 Farrer, 1966, p. 53.
15 Farrer, 1966, p. 57.
16 Farrer, 1966, p. 58.
17 Farrer, 1966, p. 70.
18 Farrer, 1966, p. 104.
19 Farrer, 1966, p. 125.
20 Quoted in Wroe, 1992, p. 41.
21 Matthew 8.3.
22 Mark 2.12.
23 Luke 8.52.
24 John 11.34, 38.
25 Revelation 21.4.
26 Genesis 1.28.
27 Romans 5.17, 2 Timothy 2.12, Revelation 5.10.
28 Farrer, 1966, pp. 169–70.
29 Wolterstorff, 1987, p. 31.
30 From a spiritual, quoted by Sandra Wilson in Wilson et al., 1986, p. 13.
31 Farrer, 1962, p. 53. Cf. Lloyd, 1998, p. 149.
32 Farrer, 1962, p. 53.

33 E.g. Williams, 2001, p. 267. This is a revised version of the answer I gave to the same question in Lloyd, 1998, p. 149.

34 Milbank, 1990, p. 390.

35 Isaiah 11.6–9.

36 For more on this, see Lloyd, 1998, p. 148.

37 Cf. Lloyd, 1998, p. 149.

38 Farrer, 1966, pp. 58–9.

39 Ward, 1969, pp. 251–4. For further discussion of the debate between Ward and Hick, which is the context of this quotation, see Lloyd, 1996, pp. 66–8, some of which is used here.

40 Ward, 1970, p. 231. Hick says in his reply to Ward (Hick, 1970) that he is not subscribing to the Platonic dictum which Ward attacks (but see Hick, 1957, p. 171). His position is not that once God reveals himself we are necessitated to return to him, but that our nature is inwardly structured towards him, so that we will find at the same time our own perfecting and our own right relationship to God. His argument against a free fall without epistemic distance is, then, presumably that, given our being inwardly structured towards God, our falling away from God would be incomprehensible. But to be that strongly structured towards God would seem to be close to the hypnotist–patient analogy which Hick sees as incompatible with a genuine relationship between God and human beings. It would seem to deny the very human freedom upon which Hick's argument at other points relies.

41 Cf. Lloyd, 2018a, p. 268.

42 Polkinghorne, 2003, p. 47.

43 Moltmann, 1985, p. 87.

44 Cf. Williams, 2001, p. 267. I develop this argument in more depth in Lloyd, 2018a, pp. 268–9.

45 See Cullmann, 1958 and Brown et al., 1998.

46 See Wright, 1999.

47 Isaiah 11.6–9.

48 Farrer, 1966, p. 60.

49 Farrer, 1966, p. 128.

50 On the theological importance of the physicality of the Resurrection, see most recently Levering, 2019, who presents a strong theological case against the impulse to make the Resurrection more plausible by spiritualising it. For the physicality of Jesus' resurrection within its first-century historical context, see Wright, 2003.

51 1 Peter 2.9.

52 Farrer, 1966, p. 12.

53 Lloyd, 2018a, 2018b.

Austin Farrer and C. S. Lewis

JUDITH WOLFE

C. S. Lewis returned to Christianity in 1931, the same year that Farrer returned to Oxford from his curacy in West Yorkshire to become chaplain and tutor at St Edmund Hall. We do not know when they met; the first record of joint endeavours comes from Trinity Term 1942, when Austin Farrer (by then chaplain and tutor at Trinity College) gave his first talk at the Socratic Club, over which Lewis presided. The talk was entitled 'Did Christ rise from the dead?' A few months later, Lewis gave the first of several sermons on miracles in London, centring on the miracle of Christ's resurrection. This eventually grew into his book *Miracles*.[1]

Lewis and Farrer became trusted colleagues. When Lewis was writing the radio talks that eventually became *Mere Christianity*, he circulated the manuscripts to representatives of the major branches of Christianity, and it is thought that Farrer was his Anglican *censor libri*.[2] From 1942 until Lewis's move to Cambridge, Farrer spoke at Lewis's Socratic Club 16 times – fewer only than Lewis himself.[3] The Socratic Club remained their main meeting place for ten years. Lewis's closest 'circle' was, of course, the Inklings; and it is perhaps of interest that Farrer, despite the poetic mind that John Hick so rightly praises in his foreword to *A Reflective Faith*, did not attend Inklings meetings. Farrer was, however, in Basil Mitchell's later account, 'the central figure' of the Metaphysicals, which Rob MacSwain calls the philosophical counterpart to the more literary Inklings. Founded in 1946 by Eric Mascall at Christ Church, the Metaphysicals were a group of mostly Anglican philosophers and theologians who, according to Mitchell, 'shared a common dissatisfaction with the restrictions which tacitly governed philosophical discussion at a time when "metaphysical" was the rudest word in the philosopher's vocabulary'.[4] (Mitchell adds that 'indeed a major reason for the rest of us in the early days to go on meeting was to make sure that Farrer continued to work seriously in philosophy and not spend too much of his time in New Testament exegesis'.[5]) Lewis was not of their number, though Professor Diogenes Allen of Princeton Theological Seminary reports that Lewis attended at least one meeting of the Metaphysicals at which Allen himself was also present,[6] and Basil Mitchell suggests that he may have attended others.[7]

The Socratic Club seems to have been an important intersection of Inklings and Metaphysicals, and it was a Metaphysical, Basil Mitchell, who succeeded Lewis as the club's second president.[8] Farrer, in a now-famous account of the Socratic Club, recalls Lewis's and his joint endeavours there:

> [Lewis] was a bonny fighter. His writing gave the same impression as his appearances in public debate. I was occasionally called upon to stop a gap in the earlier programmes of Lewis' Socratic Club. Lewis was president, but he was not bound to show up. I went in fear and trembling, certain to be caught out in debate and to let down the side. But there Lewis would be, snuffing the imminent battle and saying 'Aha!' at the sound of the trumpet. My anxieties rolled away. Whatever ineptitudes I might commit, he would maintain the cause; and nobody could put Lewis down.[9]

There are other contexts in which Farrer and Lewis might have been expected to meet but did not, and indeed their association seems not to have been very close until the 1950s. For example, Lewis does not seem to have attended Farrer's 1948 Bampton Lectures,[10] and only engaged Farrer's work widely the following decade. He did not read *The Rebirth of Images*,[11] and Farrer's books in Lewis's library all date from the 1950s and 1960s: *Lord I Believe* (1955), *A Short Bible* (1956) and

Saving Belief (1964).[12] The latter two carry his blurbs. Of his other works, Lewis notes that he has read *Love Almighty and Ills Unlimited* (1961) 'with great enjoyment'.[13]

The main catalyst for a warmer and more intimate association seems to have been Joy Davidman. Austin and Kay were one of the few couples in Oxford to have made friends with Jack and Joy as a couple, and Kay became one of Joy's closest friends. Austin was one of the witnesses at Lewis and Joy's civil marriage of convenience at the Registry on St Giles in 1956. In 1960, he gave Joy the sacrament of reconciliation on her death-bed, and she asked him to read her funeral service, which he did at the Oxford Crematorium. There is a touching letter from Lewis to Austin and Kay a week after Joy's death, telling them that Joy had asked him on her deathbed to give her fur coat to Kay. 'I know it's far too big for her', she said, 'but she could use it as a present for someone else.'[14] And Lewis adds: 'She loved you both very much. And getting to know you both better is one of the many permanent gains I have got from my short married life.' That year, Lewis dedicated *Reflections on the Psalms* to Austin and Kay.

Lewis admired the Farrers' hospitality and refinement. Walter Hooper, Lewis's private secretary in his last year of life, recalls how in 1963, when Lewis and he had Austin and Kay over for tea at the Kilns, Lewis said afterwards: 'It was like entertaining elves.' In July that year, Lewis was hospitalised with a heart attack, and it was Farrer whom the doctors informed, along with Lewis's stepson Douglas and Walter Hooper. It was also Farrer to whom Walter brought Lewis's parish priest, Ronald Head, to discuss his condition. In November of that year, Farrer gave Lewis the last sacraments while in hospital. His funeral – a very private affair – was conducted by the vicar of Holy Trinity Headington, who had been Lewis's parish priest since 1952. Austin read the lesson. At the much larger Memorial Service in the Chapel of Magdalen College the following month, he preached the memorial sermon, which is collected in Farrer's sermons.[15]

This is about as much as can be gleaned about Lewis and Farrer's personal association from extant written sources.

Their joint ventures in the Socratic Club and their comments on each other's work make clear how important mutual encouragement and support was to both, particularly in an Oxford increasingly inhospitable to their way of thinking. But it is that way of thinking itself – sufficiently close that it might without exaggeration be called a joint intellectual legacy – which is the most interesting aspect of their association. A number of (mainly posthumously) published evaluations of each other's thought provide a good starting point for assessing that legacy.

Lewis's responses to Farrer, both in print and in correspondence, are almost unreservedly positive. Although Lewis gave Austin's wife Kay relatively detailed criticisms of her fiction, only one minor criticism of Austin is recorded.[16] This is probably due mainly to the fact that Kay's work fell within Lewis's professional purview as a literary critic. It is strictly as literature that he critiqued her work, offering such retorts as the complaint that one of her figures 'speaks like a Charles Williams character'. Austin's work, by contrast, was beyond Lewis's expert criticism, because it was that of a professional philosophical theologian, which Lewis keenly knew himself not to be. This does not mean that Lewis was not sometimes school-masterish in his off-hand appraisals: in 1949, having read *The Glass of Vision*, he noted in a letter to Sister Penelope, 'I think he is alpha +'.[17] But generally, he assumed the position of a learner. One of Lewis's most amusing remarks is also the most telling in this regard. Reading Farrer's introduction to his *Short Bible*, Lewis immediately wrote to Kay: 'I don't know that I ever got so much from so few pages before: deepest problems disarmed with a turn of the wrist. If only real theologians like him had started doing *oeuvres de vulgarisation* a little earlier, the world wd. have been spared C. S. L.'[18]

In his published endorsements of Farrer's work, Lewis celebrated Farrer's intellectual brilliance and spiritual maturity, and the distinctive restraint and grace that flowed from it. In 1960, he wrote a preface for *A Faith of Our Own*, the US edition of *Said or Sung*. (As Rob McSwain notes, a similar fate of re-titling befell Archbishop Michael Ramsey's history *From Gore to*

Temple – that is, from Charles Gore to William Temple – the same year. The American publisher renamed the book *An Era in Anglican Theology* due to concerns that American readers might think a book entitled *From Gore to Temple* was about Old Testament animal sacrifice.) Lewis's praise is worth quoting, both for its aptitude and for what it reveals about what Lewis valued. It notes that books like this are rare, because it is not often that a theologian of such learning comes to us 'simply as a priest', combining such theological depth with such simplicity of expression. Farrer's sermons, Lewis writes,

> lead us through a structure of thoughts so delicately balanced that a false word, even a false tone, might land us in disaster. Opposite errors threaten from both sides, so that the author has to tread a path as narrow as a hair. Yet I believe the simple reader will be perfectly capable of following them and will remain quite unaware of all the shoals and rocks that have been avoided. When the author was really dancing among eggs, he will seem to have been strolling across a lawn.[19]

The image is as characteristic of Lewis as it is descriptive of Farrer. And Lewis concludes, shrewdly and with a hint of self-criticism:

> Perhaps, after all, it is not so difficult to explain why books like this are rare. For one thing, the work involved is very severe; not the work on this or that [piece] but the life-long work without which they could not even have been begun. For another, they demand something like a total conquest of those egoisms which – however we try to mince the matter – play so large a part in most impulses to authorship. To talk to us thus Dr Farrer makes himself almost nothing, almost nobody. To be sure, in the event, his personality stands out from the pages as clearly as that of any author; but this is one of heaven's jokes – nothing makes a man so noticeable as vanishing.[20]

Lewis loved this appearance of self-forgetting in Farrer until the last. On *Love Almighty and Ills Unlimited*, he wrote to his friend: 'You once said that you wrote with difficulty, but no one would guess it: this is full of felicities that sound as unsought as wildflowers . . .'[21]

Farrer's appraisals of Lewis were more detailed and critical. They are contained primarily in two texts: 'In His Image', the 1963 memorial sermon he preached in Lewis's honour; and 'The Christian Apologist', an assessment written shortly after Lewis's death for a collection published by his editor, Jocelyn Gibb.[22] Both texts make clear that Farrer did not regard Lewis as a philosopher, and only to some extent as a theologian. This was not intended as a disparagement, but as a professional observation. Academic philosophy, Farrer noted, is 'an ever-shifting, never-ending public discussion, and a man who drops out of the game drops out of philosophy'. Lewis, he thought, did to a significant extent drop out. Following the end of his philosophical education in the mid-1920s, he never became 'quite at home in what we may call our post-positivist era'. As a consequence, Farrer did not think that Lewis's

philosophical commendations of theism [could] usefully be recommended to puzzled undergraduate philosophers of the present day. His literary, his moral, and his spiritual development was continuous; his philosophical experience belonged to the time of his conversion.[23]

Farrer cites the example of Lewis's philosophical idealism, manifesting itself in a construal of humans primarily as intellectual agents with a moral will. This understanding, Farrer thought, led Lewis to underestimate 'the full involvement of the reasonable soul in a random and perishable system', and so distorted his approach to such things as the problem of pain.[24] Farrer himself was much readier than Lewis to attribute human suffering to evolutionary vicissitudes, and to acknowledge that the 'cross-accidents' to which man's 'identity with a physical body' necessarily make him liable may not only attack his physical wellbeing but also 'undermine the very stuff of personal life'.[25]

However, if Farrer regarded Lewis firmly as an apologist rather than a theologian, he thought him the most brilliant apologist of their age. This brilliance lay not primarily in Lewis's ability to counter the weaknesses of his opponents, though he did this with great dexterity. Rather, it lay in the texture of the vision which he presented – usually without fanfare – of his own side.

> It was [his] feeling intellect, [his] intellectual imagination which made the strength of his religious writings. Some of those unsympathetic to his convictions saw him as an advocate who bluffed a public eager to be deceived, by the presentation of uncertain arguments as cogent demonstrations. Certainly he was a debater, and thought it fair to make the most of the case: and there were those who were reassured by seeing that the case could be made. But his real power was not proof, it was depiction. There lived in his writings a Christian universe which could be both thought and felt, in which he was at home, and in which he made his reader at home.[26]

In the best passages even of a straightforwardly apologetic work like *The Problem of Pain*, Farrer finds, 'we think we are listening to an argument, [when] in fact we are presented with a vision; and it is the vision that carries conviction'.[27] It is with Lewis himself as Lewis thought it was with Milton, that we must resist 'supposing the poet was inculcating a rule when in fact he was enamoured of a perfection'.[28]

This brings us to the heart of what Lewis and Farrer owe to each other, and we to them. Both think that apologetics, as well as philosophy and theology, are at their most fundamental concerned with a *vision* of the world, and therefore address the imagination as much as reason. This agreement also breeds their most fertile disagreements. Farrer is more explicitly aware than Lewis that to address the imagination is a risky business, and his most substantial criticisms of Lewis concern this risk. Thus, Farrer argues that Lewis's peculiar merit is his 'massive entirety of view'.[29] However, he immediately goes on to ask whether Lewis does not achieve this massive entirety of a Christian world 'by living in a prescientific world'[30] – in other words, whether he does not buy his vision at the price of denying scientific discovery.

If we read Farrer's essay on Lewis side by side with his own *Love Almighty and Ills Unlimited*, written only five years earlier, we see that what he has in mind is not primarily Lewis's expressed scepticism of modern scientific practice or philosophy. Rather, it is Lewis's defence of a historical Fall and a literal devil. Farrer, unlike Lewis, regards the devil as a myth. His view is well summed up in the dictum: 'The fable of Lucifer is certainly instructive, but it instructs us in the nature of human sin, not in its causes.'[31] The nature of sin is to be sheerly perverse: 'hideously effective' while being merely banal. It is 'miserably simple' in throwing 'away the greater good to embrace the less'. Human sin, Farrer concludes, can therefore 'do all the devil can do in making an absolute beginning of evil . . . at every moment of time'.[32]

Farrer similarly regards a historical Fall as both superfluous and ultimately unintelligible, mainly because animal predation and death preceded the emergence of humans. This would require Christians either to say that the entire ecosystem of the planet changed with the Fall (as indeed the Bible seems to claim in Genesis 9) or that the human Fall was not after all a radical occurrence, for 'if the animals were fallen already, it was as a fallen animal that man acquired the first rudiments of reason'.[33]

Farrer, in other words, regards the myths of Fall and the devil as products of non-Christian mythology. In embracing them, he opines, Lewis's 'imagination has slipped from the leash of reason'. The vehemence of Farrer's own rejection of these literal beliefs is betrayed by the uncharacteristic ferocity of his description:

His readers rub their eyes, and wonder what they are seeing – Lewis wrote fairy tales but surely he did not believe them! . . . It is aberrations of this kind, rather than merited attacks on materialist philosophy, which fix on Lewis the label 'antiscientific'. What a pity it is that by such superfluous unrealities he should furnish the public with excuses to evade the overwhelming realism of his moral theology![34]

This quarrel flags a significant difference between Lewis and Farrer, all the more interesting because it is a difference within a broad similarity that distinguishes both from their contemporaries. This is their commitment to images as a central medium of apologetics – and not only apologetics, but of the Biblical canon and abstract theological and metaphysical thought as well. The use of images, to both men, is not merely rhetorical or heuristic, but essential. First, because it is impossible to communicate – in most cases, even to apprehend – immaterial realities directly, but only through analogies.[35] Second, because it is by the imagination that humans project a *whole* into which the observable facts of the world fit – and that whole, which is imaginative because it is not itself observable, determines how they understand everything within it, and is therefore vital.[36]

Within this agreement, the friends' understandings and uses of images are subtly but decisively different. Farrer selects images carefully, and traces their significance to their sources or to the constraints of language. Lewis selects his images prodigally, and ascribes to their underlying appeal a metaphysical significance. The last section of this chapter observes this difference in Lewis's and Farrer's treatment of myth, and their explicit discussions of images in Biblical, theological and metaphysical thought.

A comparison of Farrer and Lewis on myth is particularly interesting because the main source texts are a set of essays that also represents one of our clearest instances of Lewis's direct influence on Farrer. They are Lewis's short essay 'Myth Became Fact' (1944) and Farrer's tantalisingly inverted 'Can Myth Be Fact?' (1945). Lewis wrote his 'Myth Became Fact' for the journal *World Dominion*, published by the World Dominion Movement, which was established in 1923 to promote 'widespread evangelism and the founding of the indigenous Church as the natural agent for the continuation of the work of evangelization and the development of all forms of Christian work on the field'.[37] (The journal was taken over from 1973 to 1976 by SPCK as *Frontier*, the result of a merger with Blackwell's *Frontier / The Christian news-letter*.) This was Lewis's second and last article for *World Dominion*, the first having been 'Religion: Reality or Substitute?' (1941). He was invited to address a World Dominion rally in London in the summer of 1946, but declined on the ground that he was 'an arguer not an exhorter and my target is the frankly irreligious audience'.[38] Farrer, by contrast, wrote his 'Can Myth Be Fact?' for the Socratic Club in Oxford, an audience much closer to Lewis's 'frankly irreligious audience' with which one can argue reasonably. Lewis's little piece runs to just over four pages, Farrer's to about double that length. He gave it sometime in or after February 1945, and it appeared in the 1945 issue of *The Socratic Digest*.[39]

Lewis argues in 'Myth Became Fact' that myths may teach us more than many sermons about the spiritual world, partly because they consciously open out a realm beyond the natural. He singles out the elevation and awe he has always felt at the myths of Balder and Odin, of gods dying and rising again. What is so remarkable about the Christian myth, he continues, is that it really happened, without thereby being reduced to humdrum ordinariness. On the contrary, in becoming fact, that myth revealed the ordinary world as part of a larger whole that is more like myth than it is like the marketplace, or even a dull Sunday service. What to the non-Christian seems a divided cosmos – with all that is real being dreary, and all that is interesting unreal – becomes whole to those immersed in the Christian story. It is not surprising that God should have put myths in the minds of the pagans, Lewis concludes, because as their creator he would wish to give them dreams of their salvation.

Farrer's argument in the first half of 'Can Myth Be Fact?' is ostensibly very similar, but significantly begins by setting the rise and demise of myth in its context. 'The reason why myths become current and maintain their hold', Farrer writes, 'is the expressiveness of their symbolism and the importance of what they symbolize'. They follow universal lines of reason. Presumably, 'simple-minded antiquity' took them for historical fact, since humans, Farrer explains, 'were not content with general principles . . . they wanted to feel the conviction that these principles were the actual working forces of the universe; and they found evidence for this in the record that at some time the powers in control of nature had expressed these principles in one perfectly clear, typical and significant event'. Later, humans came to disbelieve in their historical truth, and philosophers began to mine them for the 'profound but implicit wisdom of antiquity'. 'The mythic story no longer guarantees the general truths, as it did to the simpler age; on the contrary, the general truths must now be proved in their own right, and the validity of the myth depends on them.'

In the work of God, Farrer claims, there is no such divide between history and myth. The words of the Bible signify historical facts; but those facts themselves signify a supernatural meaning. This is because God 'controls facts no less completely, far more completely, indeed, than I control words. And so . . . God has what really is absolute freedom to shape historical events into an expression of his divine meaning.' Thus, humans 'may construct a myth expressive of divine truths as they conceive them, and the stuff of the myth will be words. God has constructed a myth expressive of the divine truths he intends to convey, and the stuff of the myth is facts.' Farrer illustrates this beautifully by going back to Genesis 1: for in the beginning, 'there were not two events, first the speaking, then the shining. The shining of the light was itself the speech, the utterance of God; facts do not *obey* God's words, they *are* his words.'

This discussion is only the preamble to Farrer's main point about the Christ myth, which is not only myth but also fact. But already this summary throws into relief a peculiarity of Lewis's account of which Lewis himself seems unaware. Either the claim that 'myth became fact' is addressed specifically to the present sceptical age, because for an earlier age (as Farrer, following contemporary anthropology, suggests), *all* myth was fact. In this case, the discovery of myth as fact follows a distinctively Romantic pattern, trading a young naïveté for a middle-aged scepticism and then for a double vision or second innocence. Or Lewis implies that the mythic pattern comes first: that what already existed as myth later became fact, rather than being, as the 'naïve' mind would think, a perceived fact also bearing revelatory significance. In this case, Lewis's polemic requires that pagan myths pre-existed Christianity, or at least that the human imagination has certain fixed forms – forms that are usually divided from the ordinary world, but in the incarnation as true myth are reconciled with it.

This second is the more likely reading, and explains why Lewis is so particular with his myths: only a very small handful actually fit his requirements. However, this poses an unacknowledged problem for him. Lewis claims that myths furnish the criteria for what is meaningful – that is, for *what* the incarnation reveals to be actual fact (rather than mere imagined meaning). But the historical corpus of myths is much more diffuse and varied than the few examples Lewis chooses, and he does not provide criteria for determining *which* myths carry the relevant meaning. As a consequence, the entire argument is in danger of being circular. Lewis wants the imagination to show the contours of meaning, to which the world seems (to the non-Christian) to be inadequate, but through Christ turns out after all to fulfil. But can that burden be carried by the imagination, without further criteria for which imaginative visions count and which do not? In other words, Lewis claims that the world is, after all, like a story; but like what story?

Farrer is much more definite. He relates Christ not to myth 'as such', in the way Lewis does, but specifically to Old Testament myth, especially that of Adam. It is the Bible that provides the imaginative forms that the Christ-event brings to life. This claim guides Farrer's entire Biblical criticism. For him, not only the prophets' metaphors, but also the living realities of Israel including circumcision, Temple, and kingship, were not self-contained realities, but (ever more explicitly) *images* that became real in Christ. The religion of Israel always, he writes, tended towards either incarnation or idolatry; and the 'breath of inspiration' blew it towards the former. The work of the prophets, there-fore, was above all so to purify and exalt 'the image that nothing merely natural will ever be able to embody it . . . and the act of soul by which this happens in them is a supernatural act, it is the process of the incarnation of God preparing its own way and casting its shadow before'.[40] Farrer's 'myth made fact' is there-fore of a very different nature than Lewis's. It is the Bible, with its divinely given myths and images, which draws the contours of meaning that Christ fulfils and makes real.

This difference informs their assessment of images more generally. As already indicated, both Farrer and Lewis think that in dealing with the non-material, it is necessary to deal in images, even if, as metaphors 'fossilise', their users forget that they are images. Indeed, Lewis thinks that this is one of the main dangers to thought. Those who remember that *anima* and *neshamah* (or *nephesh*), the Latin and Hebrew words for 'soul', are at root metaphorical usages of their physical mean-ing of 'breath' will retain a certain humility in their presumed knowledge of the soul. Those who forget that 'soul' is, at heart, a metaphor, and think that the noun itself is a guarantee of a known reality, are worse off than the former.[41] Farrer, in *The Glass of Vision*, agrees: 'A man cannot apprehend anything without an act of imaginative creation.'[42]

Lewis's account of the significance of this phenomenon, how-ever, is more far-reaching than Farrer's, and remains consistent throughout his life. He discusses images in two essays spanning the length of his career: 'Bluspels and Flalansferes' (1939) and 'The Language of Religion' (1960). In both, he argues that met-aphors, like emotions, are the only means of communicating immaterial realities that are inwardly apprehended. 'The very essence of our life as conscious beings, all day and every day, consists of something which cannot be communicated except by hints, similes, metaphors, and the use of those emotions (themselves not very important) which are pointers to it.'[43]

Lewis believes this irreducibility of metaphors to betoken a 'psycho-physical parallelism' of the universe.[44] In other words, he believes that metaphors spring from a sub-rational apprehension of the *analogical* nature of the world, a point he absorbed early in his intellectual development from his friend Owen Barfield.[45] Farrer is much more reticent. He affirms that there are mysteries of existence that must be acknowledged rather than, as they generally are in modern thought, dismissed; and that metaphysics (which works in images) is the description of those mysteries, rather than the solving of conventional problems.[46] But he would not go so far as to say that the analogies of the metaphysicians are ontological truths, as Lewis does. He ascribes them rather to the structure of language or thought: 'all thinking . . . is a movement, passing, as it were, from term to term'.[47] In describing a singular nature, language cannot but compare and analogise. In fact, Farrer says remarkably little about the origin of images, even Biblical images, which are always already given.

And here, I would venture, we have a needed though not yet an actual legacy, namely of Farrer as a corrective to Lewis's theological imagination, which in its exuberance sometimes makes its applicability difficult. Dorothy L. Sayers called Narnia 'the Absolutely Elsewhere', and she has a point. Unlike *The Hobbit*, it could be subtitled 'There . . . but How Back Again?' Narnia's visions of noble kingship, of just war, and of a Saviour walking the earth may lift the soul and widen the heart, but it is far from clear how they can be translated out of their literary context into our messy political one.[48] Farrer's images are much less extravagant. They are marked by the ascesis that Lewis so praises in his friend. Both, I think, are necessary; but Lewis's cannot ultimately survive as Christian instruction without the correction of Farrer.

Notes

1 A version of Lewis's September 1942 sermon 'Miracles' was published in *The Guardian* on 2 October 1942, and reprinted in Lewis, 1979, pp. 1–17. *Miracles* was published in 1947 (Lewis, 1947).

2 Suggested in Hooper, 1996, p. 307.

3 Noted in Ward, 2005, p. 8.

4 Mitchell, 1957, p. 1. The book in question contains essays by several members of the Metaphysicals, including an introduction and essay by Mitchell, and two essays by Farrer. Mitchell states that the group began in 1946, his first year of teaching philosophy: Mitchell, 2005, p. 21.

5 Mitchell, 2005, p. 25. Noted in MacSwain, 2008.

6 Personal communication to Rob MacSwain, reported by MacSwain at a talk to the Oxford C. S. Lewis Society on 29 April 2008.

7 Reported by MacSwain at a talk to the Oxford C. S. Lewis Society on 29 April 2008.

8 See Green and Hooper, 1974, pp. 217–18.

9 Farrer, 1965, p. 25.

10 Lewis seems only to have read the published lectures; see his letter to Sister Penelope on 1 August 1949, in Lewis, 2000–2006, vol. 2, p. 961. (Hereafter cited as CL, followed by volume and page number.)

11 Letter to Sister Penelope, 1 August 1949, CL 2, p. 961.

12 Now in the Wade Center, Wheaton College. Noted in Ward, 2005, p. 8.

13 Letter to Austin Farrer, 29 December 1961, in CL 3, p. 1308.

14 Letter of 21 July 1960, CL 3, p. 1174.

15 Farrer, 1976b.

16 In a letter to Austin Farrer, 29 December 1961, CL 3, p. 1308.

17 Letter to Sister Penelope, 1 August 1949, CL 2, p. 961.

18 Letter to Kay Farrer, 20 May 1956, CL 3, p. 754.

19 Preface to Farrer, 1960a, p. 7.

20 Preface to Farrer, 1960a, p. 8.

21 Lewis to Farrer, 29 December 1961, CL 3, p. 1308.

22 Published in Farrer, 1976a and Gibb, 1965, respectively.

23 Farrer, 1965, pp. 30–1.

24 Farrer, 1965, p. 41.

25 Farrer, 1962, p. 113.

26 Farrer, 1976b, pp. 45–6.

27 Farrer, 1965, p. 37.

28 Lewis, 1942, p. 78.

29 Farrer, 1965, p. 29.

30 Farrer, 1965, p. 27.

31 Farrer, 1962, p. 141.

32 Farrer, 1962, p. 141.

33 Farrer, 1965, p. 42.

34 Farrer, 1965, p. 42.

35 See especially Lewis, 1939 and Farrer, 1948, ch. 4. This is a point made in detail 30 years later in Lakoff and Johnson, 1980.

36 Richard Weaver famously described this whole as a person's 'metaphysical dream' (Weaver, 1984).

37 McLeish, 1934, p. 215.
38 Letter to Thomas Wilkinson Riddle, 16 July 1946, CL 2, p. 718.
39 Lewis's 'Myth Became Fact' was reprinted in Lewis, 1979, pp. 54–60; Farrer's 'Can Myth Be Fact?' was reprinted in Farrer, 1976c, pp. 165–75.
40 Farrer, 1948, p. 135.
41 Lewis, 1939 (reprinted in Lewis, 1969).
42 Farrer, 1948, p. 114.
43 Lewis, 1967, p. 172.
44 Lewis, 1939, p. 265.
45 See especially Barfield, 1928.
46 Farrer, 1948, p. 76.
47 Farrer, 1948, pp. 74–5.
48 See the discussion in Wolfe, 2010.

Austin Farrer as a Preacher

JOHN BARTON

I

I came up to Keble in 1966, when Austin Farrer was Warden, and I studied the New Testament with him in 1967. I was to have gone on to study Philosophy of Religion with him too, in Hilary Term 1969, but he died of course just before the end of 1968, and I never did get to study the Philosophy of Religion, taking more Hebrew instead and ending up specialising in the Old Testament. I heard a number of his sermons in the chapel here, and later read all the sermons that were published posthumously, along with *The Crown of the Year* and *Said or Sung*, which appeared during his lifetime. They are still my model for how to construct a sermon.

Farrer's sermons were indeed masterpieces of composition, but at that time there was no sound system in Keble Chapel and this made them very difficult to hear. Farrer had little capacity for voice projection, and the words rose up into the roof. One soon learned to sit very close to the pulpit. But several volumes of the sermons were published, one (*Said or Sung*[1]) in his lifetime – together with the collection of very short homilies for the early Communion Service, *The Crown of the Year*[2] – and three others after his death: *A Celebration of Faith*,[3] *The End of Man*,[4] and *The Brink of Mystery*.[5] Later came *Words for Life*,[6] a collection of 40 of his shorter Evensong homilies, expounding the lessons for the day. Careful reading shows just how skilful the composition was, and this can be seen supremely in what I think is his greatest sermon of all, 'A Grasp of the Hand', preached one Christmas Day in Christ Church Cathedral in Oxford.

The sermon opens, apparently like so many other sermons one hears, with an anecdote or reflection on life in general: here the familiar experience of visiting someone who is ill and comatose, and who yet manages to squeeze one's hand, just as if they were conscious. Farrer then muses on why this is such a heart-stopping experience, and suggests that it is precisely because it is unconscious and thus cannot come from any artifice. Then he introduces a second theme, one that arises from this: our suspicion and dislike of power, of that artificial human relationships are a manifestation. So far it is quite unclear, however, where the sermon is going. Farrer is juggling with the image of the unconscious friend, the abuse of power, and the desirability of artlessness. Then he reflects on the power of God, thinking through our difficulty in feeling love for a God who is all-powerful, since such a God provokes the unease just described:

The universal misuse of human power has the sad effect that power, however lovingly used, is hated. To confer benefits is surely more godlike than to ask them; yet our hearts go out more easily to begging children than they do to generous masters. We have so mishandled the sceptre of God which we have usurped, we have played providence so tyrannically to one another, that we are made incapable of loving the government of God himself or feeling the caress of an almighty kindness. Are not his making hands always upon us, do we draw a single breath but by his mercy . . . ? Yet all his dear and infinite kindness is lost behind the mask of power . . . How can I matter to him? we say. It makes no sense; he has the world, and even that he does not need. It is folly even to imagine him like myself, to credit him with eyes into which I could ever look, a heart that could ever beat for my sorrows or joys, a hand he could hold out to me. For even if the childish picture be allowed, that hand must be cupped to hold the universe, and I am a speck of dust on the star-dust of the world.[7]

When I first read this sermon I still could not, at this point, see where the argument was going. It seems as though it is going to end in despair; and the opening image of the man in a coma, grasping our hand, has got lost, apparently – a mere sermon opener. As with a symphony in which a new theme is hinted at before it emerges fully, there are in fact little indications of what is coming: 'begging children'; 'his making hands always upon us?'; 'a hand he could hold out to me' – but one would not pick them up in hearing it for the first time. In the next paragraph we suddenly arrive, and the whole sermon comes into focus as a single and seamless whole:

> Yet Mary holds her finger out, and a divine hand closes on it. The maker of the world is born a begging child; he begs for milk, and does not know that it is milk for which he begs. We will not lift our hands to pull the love of God down to us, but he lifts his hands to pull human compassion down upon his cradle. So the weakness of God proves stronger than men, and the folly of God proves wiser than men. Love is the strongest instrument of omnipotence, for accomplishing those tasks he cares most dearly to perform; and this is how he brings his love to bear on human pride: by weakness not by strength, by need and not by bounty.[8]

The ruminations on power, on lack of artifice, and on our preference for the helpless over the powerful, all come together in this image of the Christ child holding Mary's finger, and we see (what till then we could have doubted entirely) why this is a Christmas sermon. Like a good conjuror, Farrer plants all the necessary elements long before the trick is pulled, with the consequence that when it is, we have no power to disagree with him, because he has already won our consent to every stage in the invisible web of the argument he has been spinning. And yet of course it is no trick, but a proclamation of the purest Christian orthodoxy, the Chalcedonian definition of Christ as both divine and human combined with St Paul's point about divine weakness being greater than human strength. Indeed, this dictum is deployed to show us what the Chalcedonian formula really means in 'cash value' terms: it is not an empty or theoretical speculation about the nature of Christ, but a way of describing how God through Christ shows us the love behind the 'mask of power'.

Thus the opening anecdote or image is no 'sermon illustration' for Farrer – not a way of bringing the sermon's abstruse point down to some supposed common level for obtuse hearers, but an integral part of the argument, which is a single whole. We see him working the same trick in 'Made to Order', where again a commonplace observation leads on, with absolutely no forcing, to a theological reflection on the cross of Christ. It begins cheerfully, and (apparently) trivially: 'The sermon I am going to preach to you came to me ready-made – it drove into the Front Quadrangle[9] where I happened to be standing – drove in on four wheels, and came to a stop in front of my nose: a brisk little van with this inscription painted on its door: "Crosses and wreaths made to order." The driver jumped down, opened the doors, and began getting out all the stuff that had been ordered for the College Ball.'[10] By the time we are halfway through, though, we are in the thick of some profound theology:

> Crosses are never what we ordered, but always either greater than we ordered, smaller than we ordered, or other than we ordered – and it does not matter which; for God measures the love with which they are carried, and not the poundage of each particular weight. Wreaths are never what we ordered, either; but, unlike crosses, the wreaths all have the same fault – they are all ridiculously big and splendid; because God's thoughts are not as our thoughts, and he prepares for man such good things as pass man's understanding. So the wreaths he orders for us throw into the shade all the crosses he assigns us, and it becomes painfully obvious that our crosses will never deserve our crowns. If you want to see a wreath and a cross to match it, you must go as far as the empty sepulchre outside Jerusalem . . .[11]

Other sermons begin with a reflection on garden moles,[12] Marlowe's *Doctor Faustus*,[13] caving,[14] chess-playing computers,[15] and even an old advertisement for bras.[16] Perhaps the most arresting opening is this: 'I had five aunts, who lived together in a Hampstead house known to their nephews and nieces as the Aunt-Heap'[17] – the preface to a profound reflection on the activity of the Holy Spirit, and preached, if my memory serves me, in the aftermath of a college retreat a number of us from Keble had spent in Farrer's company in 1968, the year he died. The openings are never gratuitous or meretricious, but always lead into the heart of what he intends to say. Farrer's mind operated on many levels at once, and there was no dividing-line between the celestial and the mundane, since all were part of God's creation.

II

The themes of Farrer's sermons are not special 'devotional' points, but resonate with his more philosophical and doctrinal work. There he stresses that God does not work in the world or in us by massive frontal assault, but by making our wills align with his – 'by weakness not by strength', as he puts it in 'A Grasp of the Hand'. His theory of 'double agency' points to the impossibility, when God and we are operating as one, of identifying the 'causal joint' between our wills, the divine will and the human will, because God accommodates himself so perfectly to the contours of our mind and character that the join cannot be discerned. But Farrer was clear that aligning our wills with God's was no mere metaphor: 'What Christ teaches us in all his recorded ministry is not living but dying, not how to be ourselves, but how to surrender ourselves to God, and for God's sake to mankind.[18] And it is only when our wills are out of alignment with God's that we become aware of the distinction, and need to repent:

My failures, foolishnesses, vanities, cowardices, these have been mine. Here are two angel-recorders, and each of them shows me a scroll. On one is written the evil I have done . . .

what can I do but read such a score and weep . . . ? But here is the other angel with his scroll. 'No,' I say, 'take it away; I know I must read it on the day of judgment, but I will not read it now. Not now, not here in this world, the vision of all those good things God predestined me to have done, and I did not do them: the men unhelped, the prayers unsaid, the sin unrebuked.' 'No, not in this life,' says the mercy of God. 'And on the day I show it to you, I will also show you my face, and the thorns on my head, and the wounds in my hands.'[19]

Whereas, 'if a man is in Jesus Christ and has the spirit of God, there are no lines to be drawn between what is his own and what is God-given, except that we know our good is his'.[20] And again: 'It is a paradox of language, but a commonplace of experience, that a man is never so truly himself as when his action is God's.'[21] And again,

Nothing but nonsense and blasphemy can result if we think of God's action as a rival to the action of any natural forces. God's will is the cause behind causes, and the force behind forces, not a cause or a force alternative to others. Even when God acts in our souls, he does not displace natural agents, he works through them. For instance, when God speaks to us inwardly, he does so by acting in and through the natural processes of our thoughts. And since, in this case, it is our-selves, or something in ourselves, that he wields or uses, we can in a manner feel it . . .[22]

There is a risk here, for one might ask where, then, is the evidence that there is any divine activity going on at all? For Farrer this was a matter of personal experience which brooked no doubting, but it could lead some into agnosticism:

Everything that happens, happens as though through the working of natural forces. *God's hand is completely hidden*: all explanations are natural, not theological, explanations.[23]

If God's hand is completely hidden, how do we discern it? Farrer tended to answer that we could see after the event where God had been leading us and where we had resisted his guidance; but he denied that we could feel God's guiding hand in advance – he had no time for a piety that detects special providences at work, making our path clear before us through signs. What we have to do is to obey God's general laws, and thus purify and clear our sight so that we will 'naturally' choose the right path:

> Between getting one's spiritual eyes, and claiming oracular inspiration, the difference is wide. Oracular assurances are a *substitute* for intellectual sight, whereas what we are talking about is a clearing of intellectual sight. A good pair of spectacles is not a substitute for the use of one's eyes. When I have the advantage of spectacles, I do not say, 'My spectacles tell me so-and-so', but 'I see such-and-such a state of affairs'. My spectacles do not inform me, they make my sense perfect, so that the visible world may inform me. The Christian mind quickened by faith, hope and love is simply capable of a greater perceptiveness. Heaven help the Christian whose prayers do not make him quicker of eye to appreciate another's need, and to hear the call of duty as it arises in every circumstance of life! The Christian whose prayers make him more shut up in himself, less open to the glory of the world or to the image of God in his fellows, what sort of a Christian is he? And to what can he be praying? Surely to wood or stone, and not to the living God, the Father of our Lord Jesus Christ.[24]

Farrer denied that we could normally expect special revelations of the will of God, as though we were talking with him face to face, yet he was clear that those who followed in Christ's footsteps would in practice be guided on to the right path. In one sermon, 'The Friendship of Jesus', he explains how he was saved, as a young man, from feeling inadequate for not having 'private conversations with our Lord', when he was shown the Catholic approach: '"Believe the Creed and receive the sacrament and

keep the commandments. That is union with the Son of God."
"Good," said I, "I can understand that."[25] Yet the *imitation* of Christ does take us further than what Farrer himself would probably have regarded as this rather Jewish approach, simply observing the externals of religious practice – he was in any case always clear that the heart as much as the will must be engaged. (His comments on the deficiencies of Judaism are sometimes not wholly fair, oddly in one who was so well read in rabbinic literature.) And 'the commandments' for him included above all care for fellow human beings.

Indeed, the sermons are full of exhortations to attend to the needs of others – and experience of Farrer in action at Keble was that he very much practised what he preached. I remember his kindness when I lost my grandfather, and many others of my Keble contemporaries were helped not only 'spiritually' but practically, and sometimes even financially. He often stressed that the undergraduates who heard his sermons should open their hearts to the unsuccessful and disadvantaged, including their own fellow-students who were shy or poor:

> Christ the judge and everlasting shepherd, says he will place on his right hand those who feed the hungry, clothe the naked, and visit the prisoners or the sick. It is not such people who, at the moment, mainly hold out their hands for your help. But there are among you the less forthcoming, the less well-friended, the less happy; every society has such members, often the most original and, in the end, with most to contribute to us. But a superficial and callous social judgement holds them cheap . . . but these are also the children of God; and he who loves the Father will love also the Son he has begotten. Need I say more? The contribution you can make to others' happiness – not to mention your own – by keeping an eye open for people without a ready-made social life – who can estimate it?[26]

To current taste, Farrer sometimes sounds (as he said himself) something of a 'Dutch uncle'; but he had won the right to give advice like this by his own practice, and anyway, he would have seen it as part of his duty as a Christian priest to make his flock aware of their God-given duty.

'Our wills are ours, to make them thine';[27] our vocation as Christians is to let our wills run up into the will of God until there is no way of seeing the join. But this is not a 'mystical' task; it requires preparation of our wills, not only by prayer, but also by social action. And that action must begin where we are, with our contemporaries, or else where will it begin at all? So we become God's limbs active in the world, and so (and in no other way) do we know God, as we feel his shaping fingers working on us. That was Farrer's vision for the Christian life, and his sermons express it over and over again.

III

As well as being a pastor and a philosopher, Farrer was also a New Testament scholar, and it was in that capacity that, along with John Muddiman, I knew him best. At the time he was regarded as wildly eccentric by the New Testament 'guild', as it would now be known, because of his interest in typology and hostility to form-criticism. Nowadays he would be mainstream, or nearly so: interest in 'the Old Testament in the New' is now normal, and his detection of patterns and orderings in the Gospels, thought so baroque in the 1950s and 1960s, are today far outdone in articles one can read in any central journal of Biblical Studies. What is not always realised, however, is that he combined his interest in the craft and art of the evangelists with a basically conservative view of what could be known about Jesus of Nazareth: he did not think of the Gospels as elaborate fiction, but as elaborated fact. True, St Paul was the main source for our knowledge of the historicity of Jesus' life, death and resurrection; but the Gospels preserved a true outline of his life. Nothing Farrer wrote, fantastic as it seemed to many at the time, was meant to detract from that, for unless we knew something about Jesus as he lived and died we could not follow in his footsteps; and anyway the basic facts about him were solid bedrock, whatever the form critics might say. Even a 'neutral historian', he maintained, could not rightly carp at the following presentation:

> Here, then, is my neutral story, which no one is neutral enough to write. Jesus grew up in Nazareth. He had probably attended the village school: he listened to the rabbis at sabbath synagogue. He worked as a carpenter: it was the family business. These were times of unrest: the fall of the short-lived Maccabean Kingdom had left the Jews frustrated. It seemed that the arm of flesh had failed them and only God could set up a Kingdom of his saints on earth. There were many movements of religious and political excitement. The prophet John seemed more authentic than the rest of the agitators; he called for a national repentance, sealed by baptism, to fit the nation for the great thing God would do presently. Jesus accepted John's mission and took his baptism. It was borne in upon him that the divine mission was his; and when John was put away for having attacked the prince's morals Jesus stepped into the lead. He took up the message, but he altered it: instead of speaking only of preparation for the future, he said that the Kingdom of God could be embraced there and then, would men but give themselves wholly to it in association with him. The enlistment was now; the spiritual host was brigaded under his standard; the victory, the glory would presently come. But what did Jesus do? His basic task was to take his gospel to all Israel, and so he worked round the map, outwards from central Galilee. Seeing his spiritual power, people – especially nervous and deranged people – turned to him for healing and (my neutral historian ought to admit) Jesus had gifts, great gifts in this way – for such gifts are not unknown to neutral historians. He was torn between his compassion for sufferers and the duty of preaching the gospel: the duty prevailed. People appealed to him, and he healed them: people wrangled with him, and he gave them points of doctrine: but these things were incidental to his work of preaching the gospel. He bound his followers to

himself, round an active group of twelve. He loved to have his friends sit to eat with him – but sometimes there was so much mission work to do, their food got forgotten. When they sat down to table people shared the holy bread with him whom the orthodox held untouchable. But Jesus held a curiously two-sided doctrine. Because the almighty love of God was verily present, all formal barriers were overflowed by it and sinners taken into fellowship; and so the law was relaxed. But equally, because the almighty love of God was present, men could not do enough for God; it was a poor thing to keep the commandments according to the letter; men should ask what he who gave each command would desire they should do; and go and do that; and so the law was tightened.

When Jesus had preached all over northern Palestine he told his disciples that he must of course go south and plant his standard in the Holy City; but that being the seat of power, both priestly and governmental, a tragedy could scarcely be averted. But he told them not to be downcast, because he was the destined Messiah, the King of Glory, and neither ignominy nor death could stop him from arising to establish his Kingdom. This, I say, my neutral historian ought to agree that Jesus said; he will not like it, he will make up excuses for not admitting it; he ought, however, to admit that Jesus said so. What he will not admit, of course, is that Jesus was right; for if he admits that, he ceases to be neutral, and has become a Christian.[28]

There is nothing fanciful, or typological, or intricate about this plain telling of the facts as they emerge from a critical reading of the Gospels; indeed, it is not so very far from the account offered by a self-identified neutral historian, E. P. Sanders, in *The Historical Figure of Jesus*.[29] Farrer knew all about the various 'quests for the historical Jesus' and their theological baggage, but he did not go in for such complex methodology, and drew his account of Jesus and his life and work by a normal historian's approach to the ancient texts. Note that, though he meditated and preached much on the infancy stories, the temptations, and the resurrection appearances, he does not include them in this account, but keeps faith with what a secular historian would find credible: speaking theologically, we might say he does not treat these matters of higher revelation as on a par with what can be known by normal historical methods; speaking tactically, that he does not push his luck. It is perfectly clear that for him the story continues with Jesus' resurrection. But his belief in this did not include attributing much historicity to the narratives at the end of the Gospels, since he was one of the first to suggest that the earliest Gospel, Mark, really did intend to end with the women's astonishment, who 'said nothing to anyone, since they were afraid' (Mark 16.8 – the last words in authentic versions of this Gospel).

In Farrer's account of the life of Jesus we again meet the doctrine of double agency. There is nothing unnatural about what Jesus says and does and is: he is a Galilean peasant who speaks like a Galilean peasant, though, as Farrer enjoyed reminding sophisticated English intellectuals, Galilean peasants were evidently not so stupid as you might think. ('How simple was a Galilean fisherman?' is a Theology Finals question he claimed his fellow-examiners had not allowed him to set.) He is of his time and place, as we all are; yet his thought runs up into the thought of God himself. In Jesus 'a life had come into the world which gave back to God the picture of his own face, and the love of his own heart'.[30] For Farrer there could in the end be no neutral account of the life of Jesus, because even in describing it one found oneself running up against divinity. Nevertheless, he could reconstruct the life of 'the historical Jesus' with the best of New Testament critics, and the picture he produced was recognisably on the critical map. The popular idea that Farrer was an airy fantasist about the New Testament has no foundation, and his sermons show how rooted he was in the simple study of the New Testament text.

IV

Farrer was a master-craftsman in his preaching as in everything else he wrote. Contrary to what is often now seen as 'best practice', he did not preach from notes, still less from memory, but from a full text – a benefit for us, who can now read what he said instead of having to regret that it has vanished into empty air. This was part of his conception of preaching as very much an art-form. He did not write a sermon till he had the whole of it in his head, and I have tried to show how the architecture of his sermons works, with apparently innocuous or even trivial opening remarks leading swiftly into deep theological reflection by the most natural transition. This was possible because his thought was so well integrated. His New Testament scholarship and his philosophy, which seem so disparate, as though he were two people, are in fact made from the same cloth: in both he was trying to discern the divine mind behind temporal reality, even though in very different modes. Farrer's mind tended to coherence and unity of thought, and had few if any loose ends. This could produce grand theories, as in his Bampton Lectures *The Glass of Vision*,[31] which offers a full account of the nature of divine revelation through Scripture. But it can be seen in miniature in almost any sermon one cares to pick. These sermons were comprehensible to those who could not follow his philosophical and exegetical works, and the allusiveness and poetic quality that readers complained of in those were perfectly fitted to good preaching. I would not hesitate to put Farrer in the company of the greatest Anglican preachers, of John Donne and Lancelot Andrewes. Unlike them, he spoke to ordinary hearers as well as to the learned, but at his best he could fire the imagination and move the heart. A final example will help to show this. He preached in New College, Oxford, on the statue of Lazarus, which shows Lazarus about to emerge from his winding sheets but facing away from the altar, and out of this Farrer spins an indictment of the contemporary philosophy that denied God:

Look at this Lazarus, he is your judgement; you must be Lazarus, and know from what death you are returning, into what light of life you struggle to aspire.

You are Lazarus; and if you accept the position in which you are placed, the direction of the prevailing orientation, you are struggling out of the Chapel westwards in pursuit of the falling sun. For the sun of secular truth is falling: however sweet, however brilliant that light, it is the truth of a dying world. The natural sciences set forth nature, and nature is dying, and philosophy expounds the universe of discourse, the laws of worldly speech, which will have no currency when all our tongues are tied in death. Look, Lazarus, back into the sanctuary towards the east, struggle towards the light breaking from the altar, where the Lamb of God lies slain, where from the cross and sepulchre of Christ the light goes up which never will go down, but which outshines the world: the light to which your painful eyes must strain on that day of tearful rebirth . . . when man in his guilt must arise from dust to judgement; and, may it be, to mercy.[32]

Notes

1 Farrer, 1960b.
2 Farrer, 1952.
3 Farrer, 1970.
4 Farrer, 1973.
5 Farrer, 1976a.
6 Farrer, 1993.
7 Farrer, 1960b, pp. 34–5.
8 Farrer, 1960b, p. 35.
9 Presumably in Trinity College, where Farrer was Chaplain before he became Warden of Keble.
10 Farrer, 1960b, p. 22.
11 Farrer, 1960b, p. 25.
12 Farrer, 1960b, p. 112.
13 Farrer, 1960b, p. 147.
14 Farrer, 1973, p. 30.
15 Farrer, 1973, p. 44 – this was a novelty in 1964, when this sermon was preached in Keble.
16 Farrer, 1973, p. 57.
17 Farrer, 1973, p. 62.
18 Farrer, 1960b, p. 14.

19 Farrer, 1960b, p. 21.
20 Farrer, 1960b, p. 56.
21 Farrer, 1976a, p. 126 – this is from a short article in *The Times* in 1968.
22 Farrer, 1993, p. 96.
23 Farrer, 1993, p. 7; my italics.
24 Farrer, 1973, p. 65.
25 Farrer, 1993, p. 11.
26 Farrer, 1993, pp. 64–5.
27 Tennyson, *In Memoriam*.
28 Farrer, 1976a, pp. 111–12.
29 Sanders, 1993.
30 Farrer, 1960b, p. 91.
31 Farrer, 1948.
32 Farrer, 1973, pp. 27–8.

PART TWO

Farrer in America – Four Unpublished Lectures (1966)

I

Something Has Died on Us: Can it be God?

As I was coming along yesterday afternoon to your first session, in buckets of rain, I observed the water-sprays working like mad on the grass in the City Parks, because I suppose it was raining too hard to get them turned off. I feel that to come and talk to you about the substance of orthodoxy is really rather like that. The general view about you seems to be that you are so orthodox that one can hardly bear it, and anyhow I am sure that you have an abundance of ability among yourselves to talk about what I am supposed to be trying to talk about, which is the intellectual position of our faith at the present time.

I begin with the now almost worn-out slogan that God is dead,[1] and my title suggests that anyhow something has died on us and it behoves us to discover what it is. You will understand that I am only a poor intellectual at the best and I can only talk about these matters from the side of the mind. Naturally, even an Oxford Don is also a man,[2] to take a distinction dear to Aristotle;[3] and as a man I may have my opinions about the social and psychological reasons for the weakened hold of the Christian faith in certain circles (to put it mildly). But on that side of the matter, I have no sort of right, let alone authority, to speak.

I have just been shown a very talented little book by one of your fellow-countrymen, Father Robert Capon,[4] in which he takes up this question; and he says that what has died on you is human fatherhood, that is to say, the proper position of a man in his family, and that it is because America has turned into a matriarchy (and so, of course, to a large extent has Great Britain) that the very notion of the Divine Father makes no sort of impact on people's minds. With this diagnosis of the situation I have no quarrel whatever to pick, but questions of this kind do need to be attacked from every side.

Obviously, it is no use saying that the only reason why the very conception of God has lost a hold on people's minds is a sort of emotional reason concerned with family structure and early impressions. These things no doubt play their part, but we should be anti-rationalist indeed if we thought that this was the whole matter, and that the loss of force in the idea of God that we meet with in the minds of contemporary intellectuals, for example, has no other roots than these purely emotional ones. Nonetheless, it is a good preaching line, no doubt, that people's disbelief in God is really due to their misbehaviour in some way. Father Capon delivers in fact a splendid sermon to fathers of families to take up their responsibilities, to get themselves educated, and so forth; this is a fine line, but we should not be doing justice to our intellectual friends if we tried to make out that their loss of theological belief was entirely due to emotional causes of this kind. In fact the causes generally assigned are in the intellectual field, and I shall take one distinction, that is to say I shall make mention of two factors and try to relate them to one another. There is certainly going to be nothing out of the way or recondite about what I am going to say.

I am going to start from what you all know, that on the one hand we have that sort of scientism that suggests that everything has been explained or can be explained by scientific laws based on empirical investigation so that in so far as the concept of God was an explanatory concept, it is not needed; this is a very old story. On the other hand, however, we have something that is perhaps newer and more interesting: the suggestion that a genuine ethical or moral attitude would require that we should kill God, or that we should ignore him (to put it less dramatically) if he existed, so that we might fully shoulder the responsibility of the decision for creating our own lives and creating our own world. This line of talk goes back at least to Nietzsche and is set out in *Thus Spake Zarathustra* and other writings, and it is this line that Professor Altizer is upholding in your own country now.[5]

On the face of it these two lines of thought appear to conflict, anyhow at this point: if one follows out the 'scientific' line to its natural extreme one ends up with determinism about the human being; if everything is explained by the operation of the uniformities of nature, then so are performances of the human animal.

Whether you can see these as the physical play of that amazing instrument the human brain, or whether you can see them as psychological patterns subject to codification by psychological science, on either view you appear to get an account of the human being that denies freedom and responsibility. The Nietzschean or Altizerian line, which is also that of the existentialists on the continent of Europe and here, assumes that man is sovereignly free and that there is no God except the human will. These two lines of thought give us on the one hand the philosophy of positivism which tends towards determinism; and on the other the philosophy of existentialism which tends to an almost lunatic over-assessment of the human power of choice.

Although these two lines of thought separate in theory or in appearance, I do not think we can comfort ourselves with the suggestion that we can leave them to fight it out like the Kilkenny cats, such that our enemies will destroy one another (supposing we ought to call them our enemies); for this simple reason, determinism is nonsense; it cannot be lived. Deterministic theory is a fine thing to evoke if you want excuses for your own misdemeanour, or wish to shelve responsibility; but in fact we have to live, so that the practical effect of deterministic psychology on people is to make them exempt themselves from the deterministic story they are telling about something else, themselves, or anyhow one part of their minds. I may think of a whole field of mental operations in myself as a determined pattern, but then there is the me who is adding up this psychological arithmetic and who cannot help in fact deciding to what use I shall put this knowledge of the way in which my

mind works. So the effect of determinism on people is in practice to make them think that human nature like all other parts
of nature is manipulable but if we think of it as manipulable
we are thinking of somebody up there who is in a position to
manipulate it. Usually it is me, but if it is not me, then it is Joe
Stalin and the boys, or some superior persons who will so rig
the economic and social structure and everything else, that we
shall all dance to some sort of tune that their pipes have called;
there always have to be the pipers somewhere calling the tune.
So the more the people come to think deterministically about
the human mind, the more in fact they tend in the direction of
seeing man as the master in control of his own existence, and
as the creator of his own world.

The degree to which people will go in imagining that we
might utterly recreate the human scene is almost fantastic.
There is a colleague of mine in Oxford (though I am sure his
attitude is far more widely represented in your universities)
professing[6] one of these hard subjects that get their names from
the names of old subjects, by picking out syllables and string-
ing them together back to front.

I met this man, and I forget exactly what combination of
syllables the name of his subject displays, but it is 'computerol-
ogy' of some sort; and he was telling me quite solemnly that the
greatest advance that had ever been made by the human race
was about to take place, when we had seen how to construct
electronic machines, which would invent further electronic
machines. This he described as a great break-through or mind-
burst; for when you got to that point the degree of acceleration
in the building up of gadgets would just constantly whizz up,
as you can see; once you get your robots inventing robots to
invent robots, well it is difficult to see where we would be putting all the resultant inventions but anyhow the rate of production, as long as somebody was feeding in the necessary steel,
would be infinite.

Sometimes people talk as though they think that machines
of this kind would be, or would possess, minds. This, I would
suggest to you, really is nonsense. A more sensible claim is that

machines of this kind would be extensions of our brains. Just as the power of our hands to manipulate our physical environment is extended by our having at our disposal self-operating machines that we control, so a world of electronic computers and such like things will be an extension of the human brain. The computer has not consciousness and never will have, or if it does have such, it will be its secret and you will never know; but many of the jobs that are done now by the structure of our brains in the field's memory, mental reference and combination will be done for us by machines. This fact can scarcely be doubted, and the moral of it is the same, that man's control over his world will enormously increase; and it is in this sort of picture that I suppose it is practically difficult for the practical man to see where the action of God has its place.

How does God concern us unless we think he is active in the world? Whereas if there is anything to be done now, any problem to be solved, nobody really thinks that the way to get whatever our need may be is to pray; and this is a tremendous transformation of the moral scene. People just do not think in the old way any longer, whether they are Christians or not. We may pray, if we are spiritually minded people, to be inspired and directed, to have our attitudes corrected, but not to have our needs supplied or our problems solved. Not indeed that people looking forward to (what are for me at least) absolutely frightening mechanical developments are all that reassured; and this again is something that everybody knows. Are we to expect my friend's miraculous mind-burst, or that burst of another kind, which would leave very little standing, as we are so painfully aware? Which is it to be? The matter is not under control, but it must be brought under control. Everybody thinks that the fateful decision is a question of human management or mismanagement.

Who was the English nobleman who wrote in his diary, 'I have just heard that it has pleased almighty providence, for reasons best known to himself, to burn down my house at ...... Park'?[7] Well, that could have been a perfectly serious observation in its time on the part of a man who was not what we should call a religious man – had he been, he would not have talked quite like that about the action of the Almighty. On the other hand, he may perfectly well have been a man to whose reckoning divine initiative in the matter of the fall of lightening, and the other unpredictable causes of fire, was perfectly real and taken into normal consideration.

The Russian astronauts said that they had been up into space (or somebody speaking for them said they had been up into space) and they had not found God. This is on the face of it an absurd observation because God is everywhere if he is anywhere; and if the astronauts had had time for meditation while they were whizzing round the globe, they might have presumably found God up there, in the only way by which God is likely to be found anywhere on the part of people so positioned that they cannot engage in ordinary inter-personal activities.

The men in the Kremlin thought it was good propaganda to allow such silliness to pass, and so presumably it has some appeal. Going up behind the blue to see if God is sitting up behind the blue is clearly a project so naive that one would not have thought that anybody could even be supposed to embrace it; but the picture of space-travel as such can fairly bring before our minds a couple of more adult considerations. One is the astonishing ability of man to project himself and alter his apparent powers or active characteristics by turning himself into something as strange as an astronaut; and the other is the indifference and vastness of the universe. You go up there and wherever you get near enough to a planet to find out any information about it, you find that it's dead and heaped with dust. You realise that anything that you might do to the planets which would make them seem in any way worth having, either to God or to man, would have to be done by an infinitely painful process of human colonisation up there; so you come back feeling that the world is a meaningless extent of physical stuff fantastically widely displayed; that the only thing done in it which seems to be any good, is the thing you do; the only will that can create anything worth having (so to speak), is the human will.

You could, indeed, take another view of the astronauts' proceedings. You might see the astronaut as a sort of diagram human power finding its natural limit. I was reading one of your high-brow magazines, the latest article on UFOs, or flying saucers; and one of the points that was made by the writer was a purely general one; that any centres of life, if there be any, in this unimaginable spread of galaxies, can reliably now be known to be so far away that it seems incredible that any sort of creatures conscious or living up there could possibly get to us by any sort of contrivances even fantastically conceivable to us. Turn the picture, look at things from our side, and you see the human astronaut armed with all possible mechanical power that man can contrive, defeated in the end by the mere size of the universe, and by the unhopefulness of imagining that you can travel above the speed of light. For if you cannot travel above the speed of light you cannot really get anywhere in the universe before you are dead. So that after all, what becomes apparent is that when we have exploited the potential of mechanical development absolutely to the full, we are still confined to an infinitely small, corner of space. Indeed it spreads and expands itself before our remote knowledge far faster than we can spread the scope of our action in getting round it. So that here in the astronaut you will see a sort of physical demonstration of man as the limited creature. He is a creator, yes; but of a sort, a secondary creator; he is a cunning creature, but with his ingenuity developed to the full, all the powers that are in him exercised to their extreme limit, show him after all flying round a tiny circle, which by the very nature of time-relation, he can never break out of; so after all he is finite.

It would be easy to say, and this is what I am tempted to say, that the atheistic tendency of scientific discovery and technical advance is a passing attack: that the thing has gone to our heads for the moment, but that we shall soon be realising that confinement, say to the solar system, is not essentially different from confinement to the surface of the globe. Only I do not think that this is enough, or that the problem is as easy as this.

Old religion was based on our need of the Gods: πάντες δὲ
θεῶν χατέουσ᾽ ἄνθρωποι,[8] all men have need of deities. It was
an axiom the old Greek sage could write down, because it was
just obvious that you could not control the rainfall or any of
the other things on which human life depended; these were the
sort of things you could only pray for; all men needed God. We
do not seem to need him now even to keep our own physical
being in order; this we think we can do by the aid of a scientist.
The difficulty, then, is to make out the ancient need.

If you go to a higher form of religion in which the need of
God is not seen quite so crudely as the quest for a power to
fill in the gaps in your control of the physical, you come to a
level of belief in which men feel that their true fulfilment, their
true felicity, must consist in fitting in with nature. This after
all was the ethos of stoicism, one of the most splendid systems
of thought that have ever directed the human mind apart from
revealed religion. 'Go with God', they said; not 'Get God to do
your work for you, make him milk the cow for your supply',
but 'Fall in with the nature of the universe; you are part of
the universal system, and for you to be anything worthwhile
is for you to play your part in the great pattern and the larger
purpose'.

The difficult part of our present position is that (anyhow to
all immediate appearance) this basis for an appreciation of the
idea of God has very largely broken up under our feet. Now
at long last to offer an answer to the question that I am meant
to pose, 'Something has died on us – what has died on us?' I
would say that looking at the thing from the point of view of
the mind, of people's thinking, what has died on us is something that I would describe as cosmic rationalism. By 'cosmic
rationalism' I mean that there is a purpose, or logos, embodied
in the universe and that we can see ourselves as taking our
place in it.

You may say that this would only be the beginning of a vital
belief in God, and that the next and most important step would
be a belief not only that there is such a cosmic purpose, but
that you can so root yourself in it as to live by the sap of the

universe, so to speak, and derive the life of your spirit from the fountains of divine grace. The second part of your programme does not seem to be acceptable or hopeful without the first part. If there is a divine purpose or plan, then the suggestion that there might also be divine forces to enable the predestined parts of the plan to do their work in the plan, seems to make sense. You could then think of the universe, as people have so often thought of it, as a sort of greater person with ourselves as the cells in the body of that great person. And so, as the life of an animal seems (anyhow to those who do not know scientific biology) to be one, so that the purpose and the power of the whole creature controls, repairs and uses the several parts, so the great purpose of the universe would become a source of directional grace with respect to its living part, you or me.

How strong this conception has been in the ages before us, perhaps we forget. To our mediaeval Christian predecessors the world was a perfect system, a sort of living and actual real-isation of the planetary toy, the orrery of brass rings with balls representing the planets, which the clever artificer of the latest middle ages and of the renaissance could so make that if you turned a handle, all the stellar motions would take place in their correct mutual relations. The toy was taken to be accurate; for its real counterpart was conceived to be a perfect system, a perfect machine, indestructible until it should please him who created it to annihilate it on the day of judgement; and in this system, populated as it was by angels above and beasts below, man found his proper part.

After the downfall of this pretty picture of what we might describe as static cosmic rationalism we had the mobile version – evolutionism, which still holds out in the feeble form in what is called process philosophy.[9] People thought they now knew the world was not as the Mediaevals had imagined it; that the species of things were not fixed, that man had no set place in the hierarchy of nature which writers even as late as Leibniz or Alexander Pope had described, nor was man a cog in a great cosmic machine; but still one could think of the splen-did forward march of creative principles in which man found his place. Could one, though? The more we come to know the actual universe, the more we realise that the evolution of life on this planet is not characteristic of the world and I am not much impressed by the arguments with which Fr Teilhard de Chardin attempts to soften the point.[10] He seems to say that since you can draw linear diagrams about the development of structure in the world, representing it as a straight-line advance leading up to the human brain and human consciousness, you can somehow say that the development you have diagrammed is characteristic of the universal process. He then proceeds to extrapolate and to try to show that somehow or other we are bound to reach a great climax in which the whole surface of this globe becomes one region of united social mind, and this will be some sort of end towards which we tend. But as I say, the arguments[11] amount to little more than artificial descriptions; and the predictions even if justified do no more than streamline global history. The absurd lack of proportion between anything that might happen on this globe and the totality of the universe remains exactly what it was.

From the beginning of serious philosophical reflection about theism, God has been seen as the mind of the whole world. It is interesting to notice, when you are studying Scripture, the moment when people suddenly realised that Jerusalem was not the centre of the universe. All through the early monarchic period anyhow, and during the time when a number of our royalist psalms were composed, people were perfectly prepared to talk as though God was the God of a tribe, and had his human habitation in one rather unimportant town of Palestine. Then you get suddenly, I suppose through the great political movements, through contact with the great empires, the feeling that the Kingdom of God cannot be the Kingdom of God unless it embraces the world; and so you get apocalyptic dreams, such as you read in Daniel's seventh chapter. There is, says Daniel, some kind of necessity that first there should be a world-empire arising to the south and one to the north, then one from the east, followed by one from the west. When these possibilities have been exhausted, then will be the time for an empire to come down from above, because all the other dimensions have been used up, and we do not want one coming up from below; so then the Son of Man will come down on the clouds, which means that a universal empire in the human-divine image will be founded. No one knew how this was going to be; it was not understood as a political possibility, but somehow it had got to happen, because you can no longer take seriously the thought of a God whose Kingdom did not embrace the world. When the philosophers came into the tradition, the expanding dominion of the Divine continued to expand; you could not take seriously a God who was other than God of the Universe; why, perhaps, on the face of it, it is hard to say, since we do not deal with most of the universe. Why should we not be content to deal with the daemon who works our corner of it? That might indeed have done, had it not been felt that the God in whom you believed had to have two characteristics. First he had to be in such a sense absolutely creative that you could look to him to be constantly created by him out of the ground of your existence. He must also be a God who was in such a position of advantage as a first cause that he could create you and this would be a God about whom you could only think that he had the sheer power of creation, that he was the God of the Universe, that is the first reason. The second reason is that he must be Almighty, that he must be able to save to the uttermost, though the natural system should perish, though the angel or daemon who is controlling your part of the universe should be dethroned by the supreme power. None but the God of the Universe could be this God of faith. And if this God of faith was the God of the Universe, why should not the God of faith be the God of reason? Science and philosophy studied the rational order in things. This order, then, could be accepted as the Creator's place, and so we had the religion of cosmic rationalism.

Now what I have suggested is that cosmic rationalism in the old sense has died, both in the static form, giving us a universe as a perfectly contrived artefact of the Divine Hand in which we have our place, and equally in the evolutionary or progressive form which for a while we absurdly believed, giving us the picture of a sort of escalator going up and up – absurdly, for there never was evidence for anything of the kind. One can still, indeed, call the belief that all nature is subject to universal laws, cosmic rationalism; but it is rationalism of another sort. It means not that everything makes sense or is an intelligible design such as we can conceive a reasonable creator having wished to make, or even see why he wished to make; it is only rationalism in the sense that everything is subject to an explanation by flat-rate rules. It is less like saying that there is a design on the canvas, than like saying that the random stitches there are on the canvas are on canvas; and that means that they lie on regular parallels crossing at right angles, a grid of no intrinsic interest. People used to argue for God on the grounds that the universe plainly is designed, but this just is not true; no one can say the universe plainly is designed; what you can say is that the universe, which does not appear to be designed in the ordinary sense, is subject to flat-rate universal laws, and you can indeed go on to show by sheer philosophical analysis that a universe that did not go by flat-rate laws is unimaginable anyway; not only that God would not create it, but that the devil could not.

The world, then, is not a system revealing an interaction such that we can step into that interaction and know where we are, neither is the stream of existence in which we are involved a stream of evident larger purpose moving towards an evident and final consummation or even up and up and up beyond every consummation. Neither of these things so far as we can see is true. But what do we read about the world in the New Testament? The people of the New Testament accepted the picture of their time, against which on scientific, that is to say astronomical, evidence, they had no grounds for objecting; they believed in the eternal machine of revolving spheres. According to Plato the spheres were alive with minds that might conveniently be identified with the gods of the Greek pantheon. According to St Paul (I think) the stars that (of course) for him all went round the earth, were pushed round by angels; and nature to him was a bunch of angels. But whatever the Apostles' acceptance of the current scientific picture might be, their relating of it to theology was certainly peculiar. God had made the world and seen it to be good, but he was going to smash it, that was the essential point. He was going to smash it, not only because of the fall of Adam, but also because the universe as it existed just was not good enough nor did it provide a field for the true Divine consummation. The old Age, which meant the physical universe, had to give place so that the new might be manifested. Jewish writers outside the New Testament could say that. But with Christians it had a new force because the power of the Spirit in the world to come had already appeared in this world. Thus Christianity was a religion of salvation but also of destruction; the universe was to be swept away to make a place for the fulfilment of the Kingdom of God.

This part of New Testament thought is generally held to be the least applicable to our age or any part of it. The other day among the several most interesting opportunities that I have had here to talk with various groups of people, I found myself in a seminary, belonging to a society that I would describe as just off-fundamentalist. I talked to the students there and to their professors, and it seemed to me that none of them were prepared to assert the life of the world to come at all. I know that students get pleasure from the youthful occupation of shocking one's aunts; that young men think and feel on several levels and they were then and there discussing something speculative, whereby professing disbelief they might hope to get something back from the other side. But it was at least clear that quite apart from their own difficulties of belief, they regarded this part of what they might have to preach as the last thing that you would want to preach. You could hold it as a pious hope that there might be another life but if so, what of it? We have got to get on with this one and, if we are good guys and there is any reward for good guys, no doubt it will be better for us in another world, if there is another world. But clearly this part of the traditional creed was quite inessential to any picture whatever they conceived of the grand rationale of existence or of the relation of God to our lives or to our work.

I look in another direction and I see a lot of New Testament Professors standing on their heads in the effort to think eschatologically because they have got round to the perception that the writers in the New Testament were thinking eschatologically. What this meant to the writers of the New Testament was that the physical universe was about to be smashed, and something else put in its place. The cataclysmic event was scheduled for a date round about the time when the City of Jerusalem should fall, but Jerusalem fell and it did not come off; so obviously we cannot be eschatologically-minded in the sense in which they were. Nevertheless the duty of good New Testament theologians is to be eschatologically minded, and they tie themselves in knots trying to find a face-saving formula by which they can be eschatologically-minded without of course really thinking that the universe is going to be destroyed, or that their essential future lies in another life.

Well, let's be eschatologically minded. The Son of Man did not come on clouds soon after the City of Jerusalem fell before the armies of Titus, and perhaps it is not within the capacities of most of our imaginations to think that anything of that sort is going to happen within a measurable future. But then our picture of the world is a changed picture. In the ancient mind, the mind of the New Testament, the universe needed to be smashed because it was a sort of eternal toy of indestructible parts. The bodies of the stars were made up of indestructible matter, far more noble than the matter of which our bodies are composed; nothing but a divine hammer could smash this system. There are no indestructible bodies, there is just some mysterious object of physical enquiry called energy which is not anything at all, but ties itself up in different patterns and whizzes about and has no determinate being. Our universe does not need to be destroyed by a last day of fire in order to perish, because it is always perishing. Heaven knows we perish, were it not for him who saves us. Our universe, like that of the Apostles, is an impermanence out of which rational spirits are snatched by the Divine Sower who has scattered material through the universe and seeds of life here and there; and though in Christ's parable so much of the seed perishes, yet the Sower chooses to use this process and he gets his crop. The whole question depends on whether the crop is garnered; and if it is garnered, and if this can be made a real thought, then we have a God who does something; he can speak to the universe as a man speaks to his dog; he is not like the God of the philosophers of process, who is just something kind-of-nice on the backside of the world and a sort of way of talking about how the world runs, he is a real being who does something to the picture which is absolutely vital.

Here I am simply telling you Christian platitudes, what else can I tell you? We cannot brush up the essentials of Christian theology as something new, we can only rediscover what is old, for it was revealed. That consummation towards which we look is that which gives all its decisive meaning and importance to the spiritual life here. The Christians of the first generation were not concerned with running the world, important as that might be; they were concerned with the realisation in human existence of the life of Christ, an instrument in the divinisation of man, because the Son of God had come and taken human nature so that he might associate us with Everlasting Deity, making us partakers hereafter of the Vision of God in an existence of infinite resource which could never pall.

The whole upshot of my rambling argument is that it is all or nothing. We can be as unorthodox as we like in the pictures that we paint of the hereafter. We can be as unorthodox as we like in the rejection of the conception of a last day that will be a divine intervention to smash an otherwise indestructible universe but, apart from a belief in the everlasting life of beatific vision, and apart from the willingness to preach this, the Church is not giving the people a direction for their total thought about existence which will give any proper intelligibility to the notion of a Divine purpose; and without this a belief in God has no proper bearing.

Cosmic rationalism has died on us. Let it die. The gospel is the saving power of God; it is not a rationale of the universe.

Notes

1 Later editions of theological dictionaries have a separate entry for 'Death of God Theology': cf. e.g. Richardson and Bowden, 1983, pp. 146–7.

2 For 'man' we would now say *human being* or *person*. We have left the original text unaltered here for reasons of style. The question of exclusive language prevails throughout, but we have chosen to leave the text unaltered: clearly if Farrer were writing today he would doubtless have been sensitive to this shift.

3 It is likely that here Farrer is referring to Aristotle, *Categories* 4 and 5.

4 Capon, 1965.

5 Altizer, 1966; Altizer and Hamilton, 1966. On 8 April 1966, *Time* Magazine featured on its front page the question, 'Is God Dead?'

6 Farrer crossed out the following: 'who professes some detestable subject – you know what it is like in universities now. You know that children's toy in which you have pictures of heads and bodies and the pages of the little book turn over the tops and bottoms independently, so that you get every possible conjunction of bodies and heads? This is now what you do with university subjects, you cut off all the tops and bottoms of their names and recombine them; so, to keep up with the movement, we theologians are going to have theometry, which is going to be a splendid study with an awful lot of computers for adding up the commas and full stops in the bible. But I digress.'

7 This is a loose rendition of Lord Londonderry quoted in the Letters of Thomas Babington Macaulay (22 August 1842): 'Here I learned that Almighty God, for reasons best known to Himself, had been pleased to burn down my house in the county of Durham.'

8 Homer, *Odyssey* 3.48.

9 Cf. the work of A. N. Whitehead and Charles Hartshorne.

10 Pierre Teilhard de Chardin (1881–1955), e.g. in Teilhard de Chardin, 1959.

11 Farrer crosses out text as follows: 'but as I say the arguments ~~seem fantastic and when you have stated them the~~ absurd lack of proportion . . .'

2

How Far is Christian Doctrine Reformable?

The subject that I have taken for this second lecture is the reformability of Christian doctrine. The reasons that make this question practical and urgent are human practical reasons. It is the priest in his parish, not the theologian in his study, who knows where the doctrinal shoe pinches the contemporary toe and what are the aspects of Christian doctrine that are most difficult to preach. But in this situation we all of us become sensitive to a wider and more theoretical issue. We wonder how much of what one might describe as *period junk* the traditional teaching of the Church is carrying. That period junk can get into the Christian tradition is evident to us all. There are things that we have shared and that we can see perfectly clearly to be no essential parts of the Christian truth, but simply the fashions and moods of a certain time that having become habitual have been wrongly thought necessary. At the same time we are well aware that earnest theologians, who profess an extreme concern for making the gospel applicable and revealing the essence of it by stripping away superfluities, are ready to go to lengths that may astonish us; and so we wonder where we are.

But before we can talk about the reformability of Christian doctrine we need to have some sort of definition or description in our minds of the nature of divine revelation; and so I shall begin by saying something about this. Perhaps if the very rambling argument of my first chapter could be said to have any lesson or conclusion, it was that the whole vitality of the doctrine of God depends on God being known by what he does, and on what he does being supremely identified with the work of Christ; a work having its manifestation in this world and its fulfilment in another; and that position at least provides us with a bridge for passing to the consideration of divine revelation. God is known by what he does: without his works we should have no knowledge of him at all and without his saving intervention we should not understand what he means by his works; and so clearly the decisive point of revelation is the saving intervention of God in Christ. Much has been talked in recent times, by way of setting up a contrast between a revelation of God in action (or event) and a revelation of God in propositions or statements – of course to the disfavour of the second alternative. We are told that our predecessors conceived of divine revelation as a set of divinely dictated propositions from which learned theologians were to draw syllogistic inferences. True enough; only it is really quite a long time since people thought quite like that.

In contrast to such propositionalism one is happy to say that the revelation of God in Christ, just as much as in the works of nature, is what he does. But then what Christ does has the nature of meaningful human action, and a man's words are an essential part of his conduct; not to mention the fact that apart from a revealed instruction about the nature of Christ's person and action the mere things that happen to him do not signify what we mean by an unique revelation of God. There was the most amiable, virtuous and charitable freelance Rabbi who was crucified: he was said to have come back from the dead, perhaps he did; so what? While it may be true that Christ did not talk about himself with the absolute language of Deity (it is certainly true that he did not express himself in the sort of language used by the Fathers by the time the Nicene creed was formulated) yet he did undoubtedly talk about his work in a way that set it in a certain framework and gave it a certain relevance and a certain uniqueness of meaning and of effect; and this self-interpretation of Jesus provided the basis of whatever translation the Church did when men with metaphysical minds began trying to add up the theological score. So that from the beginning revelation is unquestionably, as St Luke says, 'what Jesus took in hand both to do and to teach'. But the revelation, according to the mind of the New Testament, was by no means complete at the Death or even at the Resurrection of the Lord. He himself had promised, says St John, that many things they could not understand now would be recalled to them and expounded by the Holy Ghost in the Church; and I cannot see how any account of the basis of our faith can possibly stand which does not accept a divine concord as between the words of Christ in Galilee or in Jerusalem, and the subsequent teaching of the Holy Ghost.

We have all heard it said, often most reasonably, that there is much in St John's Gospel that does not reproduce either the form or the exact substance of the teaching of Christ in the days of his flesh. It would seem perhaps, if I might hazard a suggestion, that this author seeing Christ as the clue to the whole meaning of Scripture, writes through his lips not so much simply what Jesus said, as what the eternal word of God is found to say when the Church puts Christ's words on the background of these texts of Isaiah and other prophets which so visibly appear in John's Gospel; texts themselves interpreted by the decisive clue of Christ's saving acts. If we were to object to St John, supposing we could have him before us, that he has written contrary to the spirit of history and has attributed to Jesus in the days of his flesh 'ecclesiastical developments' as people say when they wish to be offensive – what would St John reply? Supposing he could understand what was bothering us, I think he would say 'What are you worrying about? What are the odds? I am giving you the word of God. Don't you believe that the Spirit which speaks in the Church is one with Christ himself?'

Such claims are plainly made in the New Testament, but we do not always take them as seriously as the people of that age clearly did. It was vital then, and still is vital, that the developments that gave us the Christ of flesh should be genuine developments and should have their true seeds, the germs of their growth and the foundations of their structure, in the things that Christ actually said. But the developments had their own authority. The revelation clearly reposed on a double foundation, which to them was almost one, the concord of Jesus in the flesh and of the Holy Ghost in the Church. And this, I would suggest to you, it is impossible for us to go behind. No suggestion of arriving at the fullness of revelation by stripping down the subsequent work of the Spirit to some bareness of historical discovery about the life of Christ will give us the Christian faith. It won't give us what was preached, and this is where we must start.

When does the revealing, interpreting work of the Holy Spirit end? Surely we must say 'Never', for many possibilities of sanctity, many developments of the essential Christian truth have come out in the long history of the Church which we can never disown and which we should be infinitely the poorer for neglecting. Moreover if the work of the Spirit is not continuous, then the living gospel must lose touch with the times in which we move at every point. What the Christians of every generation meet is the living, spoken word; but this is not, for faith, something different from the action of Christ in the Gospels, it is the continuity of his life in the Church developing and expounding that action.

Yet there must be the possibility of continual stock-taking and of the cutting back of errors or superfluities. Theologians and ecclesiastics have tried to lay down formal conditions or criteria that enable you to put your finger upon the revealing work of the Holy Ghost within the Church, and to mark it off from its all-too-human settings. The attempt is surely misdirected. The supreme condescension of God, we may sometimes think, is not seen even in the saving incarnation, for there the Divine Action clothes himself with a manhood that in using he makes perfect; but in the condescension by which the Spirit of God takes on the very forms of being and action belonging to redeemed but most imperfect creatures. This can only mean that speaking theologically – looking at the thing from the point of view of the Divine Action – we must be ready to attribute to the Spirit of God just as much that winnowing process that gradually blows off the chaff, that slow, purifying process that keeps the doctrine sweet, as any positive process of further development in Christian thought or practice. And so for us to occupy this sort of position (I say 'us', for I dare say something like what I have said will hardly be unacceptable to you), there is a very difficult piece of judgement or of understanding constantly to be exercised. While it's folly and death to strip everything down, to cut back to the beginnings and leave them naked, at the same time the Church has constantly to be cutting back to the beginning and testing the legitimacy or the truth of later developments by that beginning; for after all our faith rests on an act of sheer revelation so that the mere criteria of enlightened conscience, scientific reason, or philosophical clarification are insufficient for controlling the ongoing development of Christian doctrine. It is necessary for us to be constantly sure that the developments are proper developments, that we are being true to our title-deeds; and this is something that can hardly be done by any kind of dead-reckoning. One can see whether the result of a piece of mathematical calculation genuinely follows from the basic equations, or whatever initial formulae were taken. But there is no sort of dead-reckoning of that kind by which it can be seen that Christian developments are legitimate; it requires judgement and the gift of the Spirit of God to see these things, just as much as it does positively to interpret or freshly to apply saving truth.

It seems as though there is bound to be a sort of swing of the pendulum about this matter. Sometimes we shall be rejoicing in the riches of our historical inheritance, in the fullness (as we say) of Catholic truth; at other times we shall be looking for the unity of it all in the simplicity of the gospel. These two movements are perfectly right and necessary, and it is inevitable no doubt that in any given time the pendulum should be swinging more this way or more that way. When I was a lad coming from that simple Protestantism, which I gather is the background of so many Americans, what intrigued my friends and me, and uplifted us, was this thought of the fullness of the Catholic truth. At present the swing is unquestionably the other way.

If you were to take different Christian confessions you might say that the Protestant bodies are on the whole committed to the constant search after primitivity. Of course being human establishments they develop their own tradition and even glory in it; but if you can characterise them, primitivism is their line; while the Roman Catholic Church is supposed to be committed to the fullness of catholic faith; and we Episcopalians are as usual tortured by being suspended in between the two; only that position of torture is, I would have thought, the position of the truth. One seeks refuge from one's perplexities by opting for some extreme when really one has got to face this curious dialectic, this recognition of an expanding truth which has constantly to be criticised. The Spirit is at work, and we hope we can make ourselves his instruments. We are always imperfect instruments, and the fact that we hope he uses us does not let us off any of the sweat or agony of our position.

In our time, just as Protestant bodies grow a sort of moss of tradition, not always of the highest vegetative quality, so Romanism in effect has to cut back. The theoretical position of the Roman hierarchs is one that causes them, like Shaw's hero in 'Arms and the Man', to fold their arms and say, 'I never apologise, I never withdraw'. But in fact they have a way of getting around their own firm positions by just forgetting them and concentrating their attention on other matters, or else by way of dispensation. 'All Catholics fast for the weekdays in Lent', we used to hear 'except heavy manual workers, the old, the young, mothers of families . . .', and in the end it turned out that only members of religious orders were bound by the fast at all. You keep the front door firmly shut but then there is an awful lot of traffic that goes on out of the scullery window; such is the method.

We all ought to take with the greatest seriousness what has been going on in Rome lately, but looked at in a certain view it appears to be somewhat comic. They have decided, as far as I can make out, that the infallible Pope will be just as infallible if he acts with a Council as if he acts without one. Is not this comedy? If he is infallible anyhow, why bother with the Council? But we all know what the practical effect is that no Pope will ever try to go it alone again; because if there are those two alternative methods of making such pronouncements on faith and morals as the Church needs to have made decisive and which the next generation may consider infallible, no Pope is ever again going to prefer the solo performance; so that one sees how Romanism, while in theory it does not apologise and does not withdraw, can in fact get round even infallible decisions like that which made the infallible Pope – I am sorry I have gone off on a digression.

The business of cutting back to the primitive which is going on now can perhaps most easily be illustrated not from doctrine but from liturgy. We are all at present trying to cut back in that field and we think it a fine thing. Of course priests ought to celebrate communion facing the people, and where it is possible something called concelebration should take place; everybody should be gathered round the table, excessive solemnities should be cropped, and so on. Such is the modern mood. In the Middle Ages they developed a different sort of symbolism according to which the chancel of the church represented heaven and the white robed clerics the angels and they were facing towards the presence of God; and so the priest looked upwards above the altar as it were into the face of his Creator, and all the people were behind him. This was the Godward offering and why it is held so obvious that it was superstitious or illegitimate while more primitive developments (which were already developments) were in accordance with the spirit of the gospel, I do not know. What is evident is that in cutting back to primitivity, as people think, they always are in fact acting with a view to contemporary needs. The reason why we think that the primitive liturgical forms are so much better than the medieval is that they happen to fit in better with the contemporary mood; and this may be a very good reason for going back there. Admittedly liturgy isn't doctrine and I will allow it is not so solemn a matter; so long as you do not say that when I celebrate the sacrament in Keble Chapel Oxford, with my face towards the east, I am being very wicked.

When doctrine is under reform by a cut-back to the primitive, as happened (in the belief of radicals) at the Reformation time (and after all they did find out a few things about the New Testament which had been ignored in the Middle Ages), contemporary moods are always making themselves felt, as obviously at the Reformation time the upsurge of individualism was felt all over Europe. There is nothing remarkable about the interplay of historical perceptions and contemporary influences. Why, if you even set out to write the history of times before your own, you always borrow the categories of your historical study from your own time, and this influences your presentation. It does not, of course, mean that you cheat or try to persuade the facts because of your modern interests. Nowadays people sit down to perform the very difficult task of writing an economic history (say) of the Roman Empire, a highly interesting subject. The ancients themselves never used such categories at all: they were almost unaware of economics, though they were sometimes desperately aware of a monetary problem. If, then, you write an economic history of the ancient world, you are not writing a history of things as they saw them; you are talking about human life, but not human life as they knew they were living it. On the other hand if we ask modern questions of the ancient facts we don't force the answer; to write an economic history of the ancient world is not to start with the intention of proving Keynesian economics or anything of that kind – at least let us hope not; if you do it is not history. But however scrupulously we are in response even to study something so arid and objective as the economics of the ancient world is to impose categories and to ask questions in terms of which our answers will be given.

Similarly whenever we look at the origin of the Christian faith, since we cannot simply place ourselves in a first-century museum and condition ourselves absolutely to think first-century thoughts, we are always seeing the facts from the point of view of our own interests and needs; and so with the individualism of the men at the Reformation time, their desperate need for a sense of assurance and individual salvation. Their problem was not the human problem as it presented itself to St Paul; you can read it into him, or indeed you can get true answers to a sixteenth-century question out of him; you can determine on which side of a fence you put up the Apostle comes down. But what is new I think in our situation is that we don't even try to make contemporary categories obedient tools – tools with which to criticise current theological opinion in point of consistency with itself, accepting tradition by asking whether it is true to itself, tolerable to common reason or fidelity to its origins; we make them not our tools but our masters. We want them not simply to supply us with the questions we ask, but to determine within what limits we will tolerate the answers we get. That this is so, you must of course be aware. For example, would-be Christians now approach the gospel fact with the conscious assumption that there cannot be any miracles, the revelation cannot be supernatural; for God works no doubt through the world, but any question of an intervention, on his part, depending perhaps on miraculous events, is ruled out because the modern mind will not have this. To find Christians reasoning like this is surely unique in the history of our religion. I call it new – it began presumably in the eighteenth century, and on and off it has been working up until now.

I say that our enforcing of modern categories is conscious; but you will find ingenious Germans and their disciples tying themselves in knots to prove that the contemporary criteria that they are imposing on the primitive revelation really spring out of that revelation itself. A citizen of yours wrote a book, which I thought I had better look at as I was coming this way, to see what was being said. Have you noticed how these men, when they are going to try to get away with something quite outrageous, quote Latin tags from Luther or from Calvin? The phrases somehow have the ring of eternal truth; quote enough of them and you can get away with murder. The example that struck me was this: the author I allude to had set his heart on extending to the mediatorship of Christ the criticism some of our brethren bring against the intervention of the Christian priest 'between God and me'. You might think that it was an unhopeful attempt, to find gospel grounds for cutting Christ out. But he didn't shrink from this endeavour. He argued his position on the gospel principle of *sola gratia*: everything must be by grace alone, nothing must be conditioned by anything such as my direct concern or involvement with the historical person of Jesus, or the events of his life and death; these may have been events that *de facto* launched the true spiritual religion into the world and it may be very profitable to repeat to ourselves the knowledge of them, but if we were to say we were attached to Christ in an unique and as it were sacramental way we should be conflicting with the principle that all is by the free grace of God. Well, bless my soul, isn't it clear that what the man is doing here is standing the gospel preaching on its head? *Sola gratia* is a Pauline principle, if it is anything. St Paul was far more clear that salvation was by Christ and Christ alone and by membership in Christ, than he was that the proper way of laying hold of Christ is faith, or that the action of God in Christ is sheer grace. These are corollaries read out of the fact; the fact is Christ, not justification, not *sola gratia* or *sola fides* or any of these reformation slogans. But as I say, if you see a man talking like this (I can only say, so absurdly, if he regards himself as an interpreter of the New Testament), you see to what lengths people will go to try and find within the Christian tradition itself and its true origins a justification for rationalistic criteria which they are imposing on the facts because these are part of the stuff of the modern mind.

However great our concern may be with making the gospel applicable, we cannot accept the proposition, 'You *must* be a contemporary man, you *may* be a Christian if you can', which seems to be the basis of this sort of thinking. On the contrary, though in a sense I cannot help being a modern man, because here I am, I *must* be a Christian because Christ has laid hold of me; I *must* judge contemporary-mindedness from a Christian standpoint. At the same time I cannot shut myself up in any single traditionalist formula, for I have to admit, as I began by saying, that the action of the Holy Ghost is one of winnowing the grain as well as raising the crop; and so I have got to think about these things, to wrestle with these difficulties in which

I find myself as a modern trying to understand my Christian tradition. I have got to think about these things, and I have got to judge.

To take up a splendid cry, the gospel must be demythologised. Now what does that mean? The gospel must be demythologised, for myth is to most of us a bad word, though G. K. Chesterton tried to rehabilitate it. Never mind him, let it go. If myth is a bad word then it means some sort of imaginative falsification, or else, of course, it can mean just plainly a false story. Well now, when one says that the Christian tradition has to be demythologised one may be pointing out that the Christian tradition has at various times picked up false stories. The tales about the corporeal assumption of the Virgin into heaven are legends that only appeared long after the pretended events; and these are false stories. You can have a purified doctrine about Mary's admission to the final state in body and spirit in the same sense in which we hope to enjoy the final state of our perfection in body and spirit, whatever that may mean. But there is unquestionably underlying the tradition of her assumption a silly tale, vainly invented. On the other side, the side of imaginative falsification, the true substance of the gospel will have to be demythologised and always is being demythologised from age to age, if that means the abandonment of parabolic or figurative expressions descriptive of the facts, which people no longer find meaningful. The Son of God did not 'come down from heaven' literally, for before he was incarnate he was in no place, he only had a place by incarnation; so he could not come from anywhere to anywhere. But he did take human existence. One could easily multiply similar examples.

If we look at the work of the arch demythologiser,[1] we shall see that in fact what he is calling for is neither the dropping of tales for which there was never any sort of evidence, nor the reinterpretation of figurative descriptions of supernatural events, but the taking out of the supernatural entirely. Now this I think is the quarrelling point, and this is where we have to make a stand. Does the modern mind reject the supernatural?

By the supernatural, properly speaking, we don't mean the spooky or miraculous or preternatural; what we mean is strictly the setting up from God's side of special bonds between his existence or action and ours, thereby introducing into our lives principles of action and bonds of relationship that are supernatural to us, that is, outside our natural capacity and inborn powers as creatures. Perhaps you do not think so, but when I consider the task that it seems to me is incumbent upon us, of constantly rethinking our tradition and winnowing out the chaff, and retesting it by its origins, it seems to me plain that the supernatural in this sense is the core, the heart of the whole thing. You can interpret the person of Christ in many ways, but what used to be called naturalism is destructive of Christianity. Not only was Christ a supernaturalised man but insofar as we have union with him in his mystical body, we are supernaturalised, and our supernaturalisation will take full effect and become plain in another world. We know not how we shall be, but we know we shall be like him, for we shall see him as he is [cf. 1 John 3.2].

This is my *articulus stantis vel cadentis ecclesiae*[2] for the moment, not justification by faith, as Luther made it. Perhaps that was the critical article then, but it seems to me that the critical article now is the supernatural in the sense I have defined. How to talk about the supernatural is very difficult, but not only are we bound to believe that God is supernatural to us, and therefore has to be talked about under figures or similitudes that are never literal, but we are also going to believe that by special acts he adds a supernatural dimension to human existence, primarily to Christ, secondarily in us, more evidently in saints and fully in the state of glory. Without this, everything goes. Or no, you still have something, only it is not Christianity.

Supposing one takes a test-case. Were the fathers of the Church demythologising in the way that is now demanded, when they defined the Blessed Trinity and the Person of Christ? They found in the scripture a multitude of figures descriptive of the special standing of Christ in relation to God, and the special and divine nature of his work. These they set out to reduce. They in fact took as the categories of their explanation just *being*, and *personal being*. God is a perfectly blessed and self-sufficient person who is all that he wills to be and wills to be all that he is. Apart from any action in creation or relating himself to creatures, he enjoys personal existence by relating himself to himself (for, after all, personal life without relation is the one thing we cannot conceive) and so he has a blessed existence in himself above all worlds. He has associated us with his life through the action of the Divine Son, for as he is a Son by nature, so he has made us Sons by adoption through associating us with his divine life. The word 'Son' here is dispensable from the exposition. Indeed the Patristic formulation is an attempt to re-interpret the fact in terms, if you like, of the barest and most absolute categories we can use; we cannot think of God but as of a real existence, nor can we think of him but as personal.

We proceed, then, to describe the Christian mysteries in this extremely pure and simple notation. What is this? Is this demythologising? No, says Rudolf Bultmann, not at all; for it is still talking about a mystery of divine action outside the world and not concerned with the existential choices that Rudolf Bultmann has to make. But I would say 'Yes'. I don't know about Rudolf Bultmann's way of existing, but to say that the Persons of the Blessed Trinity have nothing to do with our existence day by day as Christians, seems to me so absolutely flabbergasting that I cannot see how anyone can talk so. What are we as Christians, but adopted children of God? The action of the Blessed Trinity, therefore, wraps us round, for Christ identifies himself with us in setting us before the Divine Father, and inspires us with his Spirit. These are supernatural things; they are, I would have said, the very definition of redeemed existence as a Christian understands it; they do not fit into the story of human existence told by Martin Heidegger and Jean-Paul Sartre, but if so what? I would suggest to you, then, that supernaturality in my sense is the quarrelling point; this is where we will stand. Granted supernaturality, I can enter into and embrace the riches of the Christian tradition all through history insofar as to me they seem to be positive. But if after all we have got to be a sort of pantheist confining the action of God to his support of natural events, then for heaven's sake let's stop throwing dust in the eyes of the public and renounce the Christian name.

I have ruminated somewhat at large over this problem of the reformability of doctrine. I don't want to say that any of us is free, independently of the church to which he belongs, to decide what we will teach. What is, of course, so distressing to us hasty men who are in a hurry to meet the exigencies of the modern situation is that the mills of God grind so slowly. The assured positions of our faith, as we have thought them to be, took a long while to be fought out before the Catholic Church came to be settled in support of the formula that seemed best to express the catholic truth. We try to meet our existing situation; we find doctrine perhaps in the forms in which it has been given us, awkward to preach; we would like to reformulate. We are not free to do so, if this means preaching something other than the faith that has been entrusted to us by our Church and our fathers in God and our formularies then we have to wait, and by the time the Church has settled to a better understanding, the world will have moved on.

I do not know what to say about this except as a practical issue. I suppose what we have to do is to preach as well as we can those things that we can get across, while trying to be faithful to what seems to us the vital substance of our religion. After all none of us is bound to teach all the doctrine all the time, and if we are in a state of uncertainty about particular things, then it seems fair not to preach them. If people come and ask us questions, we must tell them what the official line of the Church is, and if they want our private opinion we might or might not think we ought to give it. These are practical perplexities, and they do not belong to the substance of the Christian revelation as something that is constantly developed and winnowed through the work of the Holy Ghost.

Notes

1 Farrer's allusion here is to Rudolf Bultmann, e.g. in Bultmann, 1934, 1958.

2 'The critical joint by which the Church either stands or falls.'

3

Bultmann and All That

My subject is a serious one, though I gave it a rather flippant title.[1] I really daren't say to you Americans, since half of you are Germans anyhow, what I feel about academic German theology. Of course we owe a vast amount to German scholars; they are so thorough, so *tiefgehend*, so *gründlich*; but then they get ideas into their heads. Now any student of Plato will know this is a very improper place for ideas to be. Ideas are perhaps laid up in heaven; if we manage to fish them down to earth, what we need to do is to hold them at arm's length or pin them against the wall and look at them, objectively. But once they get inside our heads there is the devil to pay.

I remember being in the University of Zurich at a period that to some of you will seem like an old friend, but to others of you may seem somewhat remote, the year before Adolf Hitler came to power. Half the people in the theological faculty were German-Swiss and the other half were Germans from Germany, and there was an utter failure of understanding between these two groups, especially on politics. The Germans complained that the Swiss did not understand something called *unser Idealismus*, which did not mean 'our idealism', as you or I would use the word, 'our high-mindedness'. It meant 'our notionalism', 'our going all out for an idea'. This is *Idealismus*, or notionalism, it's getting ideas into your head – I ought not to say this sort of thing, because it is unappreciative of a body of scholars whose contributions in seriousness and genius and hard work have laid the whole Christian world very much under their debt.

My proper starting-point is not these flippant remarks, but rather a pick-up from my last chapter. I was then talking about the reformability of Christian doctrine, and in particular about the constant winnowing process that goes on, a process that must be regarded as the action of the Holy Ghost. He teaches the Church not only by fresh inspirations but equally through the revising and judging of her whole tradition by reference to origins; and this, clearly, is what the learned study of the gospel by theological scholars is intended to serve. As I was also then saying, what is perhaps new about the present age, or anyhow about the last century or so, is that in revising our tradition, checking it by its origins, we do consciously apply to the evidence of Christian beginnings intellectual standards borrowed from our contemporary situation, and use them as criteria for what we will accept and what we won't. People have done this previously, but they did not know they were doing it. Now we know that we are doing it.

The Biblical scholar as such doesn't perhaps see that he is doing it; but his blindness on that side merely increases this danger that the New Testament writings will become a sort of diviner's crystal ball in which he sees what he sets out to see. I speak here with some consciousness because I am sure I have taken a hand in that sort of thing, seeing patterns in the gospel that I have been looking for. We all know the psychological mechanism of projection. If you want to tell fortunes, perhaps you have got something in the bottom of your mind, some sort of feeling about the person in front of you and the sort of life that is likely to lie before a man of that character, with those intentions and so forth. Then what you need is a technique of projection, isn't it, some means for getting the feelings you have in the bottom of your mind (if you happen to be a gipsy or spiritualistic medium or such like person) to come up; and almost any technique will do. Fortunes have been told by examining the lines in the palm of one's hand; and the usefulness of these lines is that they are very indefinite and that the pattern can be seen in various ways; and so by the process of projection you are led to see the pattern in the way that serves what you implicitly think, but haven't managed to bring up before your mind. It is obvious that the study of ancient documents, wherever there is any ambiguity in them or possibility of several interpretations, can be just such a diviner's crystal or technique of projection for bringing up and throwing forward what the interpreter in fact wants to believe or anyhow does subconsciously believe.

Since it would be impossible in this short chapter to make a survey of the present critical position about the Gospels, of which I dare say you know quite enough, what I will do rather is to begin at the other end and list some of the prejudices that occupy the minds of people approaching the Gospels and which reappear in the diviner's crystal of interpretation. I shall mention three.

The first is the philosophical prejudice that appears in some ways to represent common sense: that eternal and timeless truth, such as the truth about man's spiritual nature and the way of his salvation, cannot possibly be pinned down to historical facts or made to depend upon them. Just as a kind of mnemonic device to emphasise this position, I will recite you a little verse.

There appeared in Cambridge, England, a few years ago a book by four Cambridge theologians called *Objections to Christian Belief,*[2] and a little later there appeared in the magazine *Theology* a set of four little verses from an Oxford theologian epitomising what the four Cambridge theologians had said, and this was the epitome of Doctor Vidler's essay, or lecture as in fact it was:

The best of men that ever were
(So judged by his biographer)
Lowes-Dickenson was loth to tie
Eternal truth to history.

And granted our presumptuous pen
Takes issue with the best of men,
And ties the two as tight as tight,
We've still to get our history right.

Our facts are dim, but we may cite
The afterglow of gospel light,
The shining witnesses since then;
Though not, of course, the best of men.[3]

Well, Lowes-Dickenson, whom his devoted biographer declared to have been the best of men, was unwilling to admit that eternal truth could be pinned down to, or made to depend on, any historical fact. This is, I would say, a philosophical prejudice that at least wears the guise of common sense, and so Christian thinkers who uphold the extraordinary tie-up of an eternal or timeless truth with a particular historical event, talk – don't they? – (and here I am indebted to the Germans whom I so unreasonably disparaged) about 'the scandal of particularity'. It's a scandal or stumbling block to our minds, that an eternal truth of vital interest to all mankind should turn upon a particular historical event, of which, as of all historical events, the evidence is bound to be contestable; for there is no historical fact that cannot be reinterpreted, if not actually denied.

If you approach the Gospels with Lowes-Dickenson's prejudice in mind, what you want to think is that the valuable content in the Gospels, what really concerns us, is not any statement about anything that happened (it may have happened or it may not) but some spiritual principle. If this is your prejudice, then you may want to establish either or both of the following positions. First, that the facts won't bear us out in affording a solid basis for a historical revelation. Second, that our documents themselves show that the saving object of faith, which really moulded the spirituality and made the lives of the New Testament Christians, was not essentially the Man who had walked in Galilee and died, and perhaps was supposed to have risen, but was a virtually mythical figure, a Christ of faith, invisible to the eyes of any historian or any factual investigator, a wraith who sprang from the Easter sepulchre. I do not say that the Lowes-Dickenson prejudice obliges one to either of their conclusions. You might hold a high view of the historicity of the Gospels, and of the attachment of the primitive Church to the historical Christ, and be content simply to say that the Church made a philosophical error in universalising his significance. But then you would lie open to philosophical counter-arguments on the basis of evidence you admit. It is safer and more comfortable to talk away the evidence.

The Lowes-Dickenson prejudice is the most extreme of the prejudices that fill the mind of the man who, still thinking himself to be some kind of Christian, approaches the gospel facts. It may or may not be a prejudice of which he is himself aware, because as I said, when we turn to the interpretation of ancient, ambiguous and professedly supernatural books, then tendencies of thinking of which we are unaware become projected in this diviner's crystal and come to the surface; so that your biblical student whose thoughts are directed by that prejudice may not start with the conscious knowledge that he has it, he may think that it is imposed upon him by the facts.

The second prejudice that I'll state is one that is less extreme. One may say there could be a historical revelation, yes, but the matter of it would be a uniquely revelatory event, not the special presence of a divine person, for that seems to be beyond what reason will tolerate. That there is a God who works in some measure through all things that happen and shows his purpose in the field of history and human life, this we will believe; and it seems reasonable enough that some particular set of events might uniquely betray, or open to us, the clue to the purpose of God concerning us. So much we can swallow, but the injection into history of a supernaturally divine person, that is too much. What is the supposed proof that you find for this in the Gospels? Your supposed proof will be that the Christ whom historical study will reveal to you in the documents didn't teach anything like the Nicene faith about himself. He did not proclaim himself to be a divine person in the sense of subsequently defined faith; and he cannot have been so divine in any case, because he was liable to factual error in his recorded utterances.

I am going to come back and say more about these prejudices and the evidence claimed to support them in a moment. But I am now making a list of them and I am going to mention one more; and I am still continuing in a descending scale of extremity.

We may say, well, perhaps it is possible to speak of Christ as in some sense divine. But anyhow (and this is perhaps the simplest and most obvious of these prejudices) – anyhow it wouldn't fit a divine person incarnate in human flesh to act miraculously. The divinity of Christ is not such that it should, as St Leo said, 'coruscate with miracles' under the form of human life. The proof alleged is that historical analysis dissolves miracle; as we examine the evidence we find that miracle has been exaggerated and enhanced as between earlier accounts and later accounts and so we extrapolate backwards and suppose an original account that was non-miraculous.

The fact that people want to reach conclusions of these sorts because the prejudices of common sense are on this side, is no reason for refusing to ask the question, whether a scientific investigation of the Gospels does or does not support such prejudices. For the prejudices of common sense in a manner of speaking ought not to be called prejudices. They are, on the face of it, what we ought to expect to be true and it is fair enough to say that the burden of proof must lie heavy upon anybody who wishes to uphold the opposite. If I come and tell you some perfectly natural and easily credible fact, or alleged fact, you don't challenge it, my testimony is sufficient. If I tell you that I have seen an elephant sitting in the middle of a parking lot downtown, you might admit that this was a possible thing, because there are elephants, and in my country at least there are travelling circuses from which elephants might conceivably escape and go and sit down on a parking lot; but you would feel that such a statement needed a great deal of support and you would wish to challenge me and ask me how fast I was passing by when I saw this, how good my sight is, and whether I was quite sure that it was not one of your remarkably designed American cars, and so forth. So that while I have listed three prejudices – against the tie-up of eternal truth with history, against a revelation not merely through the divine hand in events but through the presence of a divine person, and last, against a divine person acting miraculously – these are only prejudices from the point of view of a Christian thinker who has already thought his way through the justification of a supernatural faith and who feels that flat common sense has been brought in where it does not belong. But in the beginning of the enquiry one must say that such prejudices are no prejudices at all, for history would become an impossible science, if we were prepared to admit miracles all over the place except on the very strictest testimony; and as with miracles, so with the other types of supernatural interpositions. What tendency has scientific criticism of the Gospels to support any of these positions the rationalistic contentions of which we have listed? This seems to me to be an ambiguous question and the whole point of the discussion turns on seeing the ambiguity of it. What is scientific criticism?

If by scientific criticism we mean the application to the gospel material of the canons, or criteria, of ordinary common-sense history, then of course you must say, not so much that the detailed findings of gospel criticism support these rationalistic or semi-rationalistic positions, as that the whole approach you take enforces them. I remember very vividly a student of theology whose faith in the Catholic position, in the broadest and least prejudiced sense of that word, seemed to be rocking on its base. In discussion with him it became clear that his decision turned on this question: ought we to criticise the gospel facts, to start with, on the assumptions of ordinary rationalistic history, and only dare to put supernatural interpretation upon them after we have put them through a rationalistic sieve? The problem was the virginal conception of the Lord. You would be bound to say the evidence here is somewhat indirect; we only hear about this event in the later strata of the gospel tradition. It is true that no stratum of the tradition contradicts it. It is a remarkable fact that the name of Joseph is never introduced into the story of Christ's parentage, until it is coupled with narratives about the virginal conception; for in St Mark's Gospel Jesus is only spoken of as the Son of Mary and the name of Joseph is not heard. There is no contrary evidence, then; but the positive evidence is later in the tradition and inevitably indirect; for here is an event above all other events most difficult to support with any direct testimony that is not open to being discounted. Well now, said my friend, if I am allowed to approach this question as a man who is already convinced that things of a supernatural kind were happening here; if I am allowed to say, I have heard the preaching of the Apostles through the Church, and have become convinced that I am in the presence of the face of a living Christ, identical with the human Christ of the gospel, and that other things wonderful about him happened on evidence better supported, such as his resurrection from the dead; am I then entitled to say that it would be outrageous to judge this question as though it were simply an unconnected report turning up somewhere of a child being virginally conceived in sequel to his mother's act of faith in a supposed angelic message?

It is perhaps of no importance, since it is only a fact of somebody else's biography, that my friend came down on that side, that he was entitled to judge this matter otherwise than he would judge a report turning in no particular context. Considering that he had evidence that he could believe, and which had convinced him of the supernatural intervention of God, he found it proper to hold corresponding expectations in his approach to further associated facts. Such was his principle of judgement, evidently a judgement of the very greatest delicacy. If you stretch its principles too far it would open the gates on limitless superstition. You must at least be able to claim some evidence that could well be respectable evidence for the fact in question. Had St Luke, for example, access to the members of Christ's earthly family? Presumably he had; this family survived and was in high estimation in the church of Jerusalem which St Luke had visited. Is there any reason why Mary should not have confided in St James (say) after he had become fully identified with the Church? There is no reason why she should not have done. The case, then, is respectable in the sense that you can lay a reasonably perfect *hypothetical* chain of evidence; on the other hand you cannot test the links of that chain. Since the Church has put the virginal conception in the Creed and it seems divinely right, we are inclined to say *Decuit ergo factum est*, it was right and proper, and so God did it. We cannot dare to use the *Decuit* outside of the field of all positive evidence;

I have no right to say *Decuit ergo factum est*, it was proper, so God did it, apart from evidence of what he did, because the acts of God are infinitely surprising and it is only after the event that we see that what seemed on the face of it so surprising, so contrary to human reason or expectation, was just the most divine thing. That is what the incarnation is like.

I have been trying to speak to you throughout, somewhat in the vein of a philosophical theologian, exhibiting to you the delicacy of the question and the way in which it is so easy to weight the case on one side or on the other; my object is not to express about the traditional faith of the Church a personal opinion that is of no consequence to you and no better than anyone else's.

I brought up this topic in connection with the question that I posed. Does the scientific criticism of the Gospels in fact bear out the sort of rationalistic assumptions with which the modern student approaches the Gospels? And my first answer is, that any historical investigation will inevitably bear out your rationalistic assumptions if you force them as absolute criteria on the facts. If you say, 'Well, but men don't rise from the dead', or 'Well, but children aren't virginally conceived', there is an end of it; you will simply be saying 'I wouldn't believe evidence on the subject whatever the evidence was'. If you go with Dr Bultmann, you will say miracle is nonsense and of no spiritual consequence or importance, that the recognition of a 'divine event' in Christ would not in any way help you to believe that anything physically miraculous ever happened. There seems to me to be a sort of Manicheism somewhere here, a sort of division of the spirit from the flesh, with which I am not at all prepared to go; but if you embrace it, then of course you won't believe the miracles.

If I did decide to push home on the Gospels as absolute prior criteria, the expectations of common sense, I should have first to decide what those expectations are. Quite apart from the special intervention of God, common sense is forced to acknowledge happenings in the historical field which were highly improbable *a priori*. It was very improbable that Shakespeare should have written his masterpieces. What I mean is this: you cannot say, 'Take a semi-educated boy at Stratford, etc. and mix in anything you know about this history or ancestry, and of course you will get Hamlet and Macbeth'. As with genius, so with sanctity. In the biography of saints, where we come down to personal reality, we come across regions of fact which conflict with the flat-rate expectations of statistical history. Admittedly there is something absolutely unique in the Gospel case. 'Shakespeare wrote Macbeth', after all, isn't in the same class of *a priori* unlikelihood as 'Jesus rose from the dead'.

Supposing we get past the lions in *Macbeth*, the lions of rationalistic historiography, and we explore the detail of gospel criticism insofar as it is independent of the forcible imposition of rationalistic assumptions, what can we say about it? Is it true that if you look into the documents you will find (for example) that as you proceed with your investigation the evidence of miracle dissolves; or that the object of the primitive belief is exposed as not really the Christ who walked the earth, but as a supernatural image imposed upon him by faith? I would say that the details of documentary and historical criticism in gospel study have no tendency to prove any such things at all.

There is a nest of false assumptions which are most widely prevalent in the criticism especially of the synoptic Gospels, the narratives that seem to bring us perhaps most close to the historical tradition; assumptions that need to be unmasked. It is assumed for example that the only way to get at the facts about what Christ taught is to break up all artificial mosaics in which his words have been put together by the author, to set them all before you as free units, individual nuggets of teaching, and then construct out of them what you can. It is also assumed that it would be proper to set aside what is evidently phrased in the style of the evangelist, wherever he can be seen to be rewriting or systematising the teaching of the Lord.

These assumptions appear to me to be utterly valueless. What is true is that if you hope to get at the very personal utterances of Jesus and the very tones of his voice, that is the proper way to proceed; you should trace back if you can the history of individual elements in Christ's teaching, and clear them from encumbrances; you should get back as near as you can to the form of anecdotes reported by eye-witnesses – it would be more reasonable if we said ear-witnesses, only we don't. But it is obviously absurd to assume that wherever an evangelist decides (say) that the matter in front of him is so important that he wants to clarify it for his readers by rewriting it in his own style, or by pulling together or systematising, he is falsifying the mind of the Lord.

There is a very interesting test case. If there is one passage in the gospel most hated by modern scholars, and indeed I suppose by modern Biblical readers, it is the prophecy that Christ is reported by all the synoptic evangelists to have made on the Mount of Olives, perhaps on the Wednesday before he suffered. Now it is plain that the wording of his prophecy and the systematic setting forth of it in a stage-by-stage advance of future events is not like the rest of the teaching of the Lord as reported by the synoptic evangelists. It isn't altogether in his style, if we can so speak; and so, since most of us hate the thought that the Lord drew a sort of map of the future march of events which subsequent history falsified, we are all eager to say: here is an evident case in which the evangelist shows himself as a primitive theologian; he has pulled together no doubt certain authentic words of the Lord warning his disciples to be watchful in view of persecutions, but he has made them into a pattern of prophecy such as the Jewish mind loved. The trouble about this very convenient opinion is that the first Christian writings that have come down to us all – St Paul's letters to the Thessalonians – presuppose precisely this pattern of prophetic expectation, and presuppose it as something unchallenged, as the very substance of the gospel. The Church is seen as undergoing the first stage of what the Lord had prophesied – desultory persecutions and other trials in which one has to stand fast; but the end will not come until the Man of Sin, Anti-Christ, has set going the terrible tribulation, and has enthroned abomination in the temple of God. Only after that will come the Advent of the Son of Man on clouds, or the Lord descending with the trumpet of the archangel (says St Paul) whom we shall meet by being caught up into the air.

Since the epistles to the Thessalonians, whether we like them or not, are the first evidence we have about what was being preached as the Christian message, and since St Paul gives out his apocalypse without any kind of argument and refers to one detail as a thing he knows by the word of the Lord, the case that we have been building up against the oracle on the Mount of Olives, as St Mark represents it, falls to the ground. On the supposition that the oracle is authentic, there is no difficulty in accounting for the special quality of its form. Just because this was to the first generation or so the essential part of the teaching, the Christian hope, it was much meditated upon. And in the course of that meditation, the Scriptures on which the Lord's teaching meditated upon was founded, and particularly the oracles in the seventh chapter of Daniel, had come down into the text of his utterance and given it a sort of form that is not characteristic of the free utterances of the Lord as otherwise recorded to us. Nevertheless, on our evidence, this piece is in a sense the best authenticated of the Lord's teaching, besides his prohibition of divorce – which has come down to us at all. Here then is a surprising example that shows us, as far as evidence can show, that the method of breaking up your Gospel material and trying to reduce it into nuggets of dominical utterance is not the only way of finding in fact what the Lord taught. For here is something that the primitive Church regarded as absolutely essential to his teaching, not delivered to us in nugget-form, but in a heavily worked-over piece of Marcan prose.

This really brings us to the more general point that, after all, the Gospels are not our first evidence for the essential facts of the Christian tradition. The Gospels are the testimony of the apostolic Church. However closely or remotely the authors of the books were or were not related to the first missionaries, their writings have the nature of apostolic testimony, in which is arranged and set out what people remembered about the Lord's words and acts. But when St Peter and St Paul preached

Christ's resurrection from the dead their evidence was not the sort of thing that happens to be contained in our Gospels; they did not prove it out of the Gospels, they remembered that it had happened, or they talked to people who remembered that it had happened.

St Paul is our primary witness to the whole Christian tradition, for he came into the Church and received his faith from the others within, shall we say, half a dozen years of the Resurrection; our primary witness is always necessarily St Paul because the authenticity of his writings and the personal stamp of many of them cannot be doubted. So it is a surprising fact that the parts of the gospel that St Paul supports are all parts that a naturalistic historian would write off as plainly the constructions of faith. St Paul tells us that Christ with words so mysterious, and historically one might say so improbable, instituted the Supper, and that he rose from the dead; and here what St Paul gives us is not stories about what it was like, but the names of the witnesses. He rose from the dead after having been buried, and St Paul clearly understands the two events as being continuous, so that his resurrection is something that had affected his mortal remains.

He also indirectly supports the gospel narrative about Christ sending out Apostles to missionise during his lifetime and telling them, as the gospel tells you he did, that they should not carry provisions with them but throw themselves on the charity of those to whom they preached. Now anybody I should have thought who approaches St Mark's story with the prejudices of rationalistic history will say that this episode has been heavily patterned and worked over from the experiences of the primitive Church. Missionaries went out and preached the risen Lord; this became the great activity of the Church; but one would have thought that while Christ was alive and working in Galilee nothing of the sort yet happened. St Mark's Gospel is arranged in stages characterised by the preliminary gathering of Apostles, the institution of the 12 Apostles, the sending out of the 12 Apostles, the employment of the 12 Apostles to distribute 12 miraculous and surely symbolical loaves of bread into lots to the crowds; and if there is anything that looks like artificial dogmatic architecture it is this. Yet the mission of the 12 sent out by Christ with instructions on how they should behave in points of domestic or economic details, this is supported by St Paul. At least, you may say, St Paul is silent about Christ's day-to-day miracles. He is. But he puts miracles and healings among the current phenomena of Christian life, and it is absurd to doubt that he traced them to Jesus as to their fountain-head.

To sum up: the current method of trying to get at the gospel facts by stripping away what is taken to be ecclesiastical interpretation from them, is refuted as far as it can be refuted by the evidence of the first witnesses that we have. And surely if there is a miracle outside the life of Christ himself in God's revelation to us, it is the appearance of this extraordinary man St Paul, so early finding his way into an unliterary and no doubt very simple sort of peasant group, so that he might write these extraordinary letters and convey to us the substance of the primitive faith.

This is an inexhaustible subject, and there is no question of my dealing with it adequately; but there is one thing I must say. How do we answer the objection (which is surely real as far as it goes) that the Christ of faith who is the object of St Paul's devotion is not just the man who walked in Galilee; or the allegation that the Christ of faith has been overlaid on the gospel person?

We can answer this objection only by a sound theological belief about the way in which the divine action unrolls. To keep to St Paul, we find in St Paul's writings what have frequently been regarded by critical scholars as two rival and really incompatible accounts of the divine function of Christ. In the famous so-called hymn of Philippians 2, Christ is a divine Son who reversed the folly of Adam; Adam being man grasped at being like God, whereas Christ being in the form of God humbled himself and became man; and here you have what you might describe as perhaps an elementary, but in principle a full-blown, incarnationist Christology. On the other hand, in the opening sentences of Romans, St Paul tells us that he is commissioned to preach the Christ who was born according to the flesh of the seed of David, but who was declared (though the word almost means 'appointed') Son of God with power miraculously by the action of the divine spirit, through the resurrection of the dead. Which did St Paul believe, that Christ was a divine person who humbled himself and stepped down from heaven, or that he was one who became the divine-human Christ at his resurrection?

The relevance of this question to the topic I have raised is I hope not too obscure. What is alleged is that the Christ of faith is a figure supposed to exist after the Resurrection, who is the object of the devotion of the Christian community, and who has been read back into the Christ of the Gospels; that while Philippians shows the reading back, Romans shows us this older position. I would wish to say that St Paul's two formulations can be seen to be both perfectly orthodox and perfectly reconcilable with one another, if we are prepared to consider that Christ though perfect in all the phases of his life according to what those phases demanded or allowed was, like any other of us, in his human being coming to be what he was to be. After all it is an interesting fact that according to St Luke's chronology, Christ entered on the course of action that brought him to his death at the age that according to the Jews was the age of manly maturity. None of us would suppose that the infant Jesus in the cradle had yet unfolded or expressed the union of God and man in Christ, for that union surely is supremely in the spirit. So that though the act of the incarnation begins from Lady Day,[4] from the miraculous conception, the incarnation itself is a process in which the divine is building up its human instrument. Christ became, was made, perfect according to the author to the Hebrews, was made mature or grown up, through the things that he suffered; and he became what he was to be as the man in glory.

If this is what we believe, then there is no conflict in our minds at all over the point that the Christ talked about in the New Testament is a glorious person and not exactly what the Christ of the earthly life was. There was nevertheless one continuous personal existence going through the several phases of his development, and in each of them showing the perfect work of God redeeming us. If we think this, then the Christ of faith is not a fantastic person imagined by his disciples, but he is that same earthly person now entered into glory. This is what they thought; this is the faith that convinced them as true, which has redeemed the world as far as the world has entered into the redemption offered, and which has come down to us; and if we are prepared to think thus ourselves, doing full justice to the travails of faith and efforts of understanding through which Christ struggled on his earthly path, then this difficulty just seems to dissolve. The Resurrection finally made Christ what he was to be, the man-in-glory: he came down from heaven and took our flesh that he might, in his manhood, achieve that perfection.

Notes

1 Farrer originally titled this 'The Gospel and the Germans', but then also noted the current title as an alternative.

2 Vidler, 1963a, 1963b. Note that Farrer's (!) poem cited below appeared in the same year in *Theology*. These are cryptic notes on the four writers in the book noted here.

3 Farrer, 1963. The verse in full reads as follows:

I
Though leaving law to Pharisees, the Pentecostal saint
May give a modest status to the function of restraint.
We do not always care to see the jaded city gent
Led on by eager hussies into free experiment;
His conduct, while admittedly affirmative of life,
Wears a negative complexion in relation to his wife.
Not of course that we would bracket such a man with the abetters
Of the posthumous edition of Miss Rose Macaulay's letters:
Oh for a heart to praise the Lord for our creative sins!

II
Press not the hypocrisy so far
As to be better than you are
Nor by confession of your plight
Wallow in obscene delight.

The phrases of the Common Prayer
Are steps in hell's descending stair.
The bars and brothels of Tangier
Make the inward vision clear.

III
The best of men that ever were
(So judged by his biographer)
Lowes-Dickenson was loth to tie
Eternal truth to history.

And granted our presumptuous pen
Takes issue with the best of men,
And ties the two as tight as tight,
We've still to get our history right.

Our facts are dim, but we may cite
The afterglow of gospel light,
The shining witnesses since then;
Though not, of course, the best of men.

IV
Objections to the Christian creed
ought not, in logic, to succeed –
Flat prejudices, favoured by
Our out-of-date cosmology.
But don't imagine you can clear
The cobwebs out in half a year;
Our abstract nouns hypostatized,
Our dogmas undermythicized
Will keep religion to the few
Another century or two.

4 'Lady Day' is a traditional name for the Feast of the Annunciation
on 25 March.

4

Does Social Structure Bow to Christian Morals, or Vice Versa?

This problem[1] is obviously a severely practical problem, because there are several spheres of life, particularly the sexual one, in which it is generally held that the teaching of the Church is hopelessly antiquated and inapplicable to the modern situation and that we just ought to reconstruct our rules. The question is in a way a straightforwardly practical question, but to the philosophical mind it contains within itself (alas for the unphilosophical reader) a whole nest of questions like Chinese boxes one inside another, and perhaps it would be better if the writer had never delved into philosophy.

The first question that I want to raise is the question about the rightness or wrongness of living by rules at all. You know what people say, that the free man of our post-Nietzschean enlightenment does not allow himself to be hoodwinked by the existence of moral rules or let off the agony of a particular decision in the face of every particular situation as it arises. If this is the proper truth about the highest morality then of course no question about the relation between Christian rules and an existing social pattern comes up at all. You must say that Christian moral teaching (if you pretend to retain it) reduces to the one precept of neighbourly love. All you have to do is to appreciate the situation in which you find yourself, and act in such a way that you do the best that you can according to your own judgement and wisdom for the persons involved in the situation, among whom you must of course reckon yourself. At the other extreme one has the inflexible admirers of the ten commandments. The view that morality is a set of defined invariable laws was of course what the Pharisees held, whether that recommends the system to you or not. However anti-pharisaical we may be, we probably get worried when certain of the laws of conduct as we understand them, and as they have commonly been accepted by Christians, are freely set aside by individuals on their own simple judgement. On the make-it-up-as-you-go-along principle, it will be thought better that Joseph should have gone to bed with Potiphar's wife; for which, I have no doubt, there was much to be said, especially by Lady Potiphar.

Before I, with my pettifogging philosophical approach, can get near the question of how far the rules ought to be imposed on the situation, or how far we ought just to look at the situation and do what we think the situation requires,[2] I do want to see what is the principle of morality; for it seems we are not Pharisees, but neither are we prepared just to play hookey with the rules. It might interest us perhaps to see what our Saviour did in the Sermon on the Mount.

The Sermon on the Mount is commonly quoted for the beautiful precepts of unselfishness and of humility which it contains. But one of the things that the Sermon on the Mount in fact illustrates is the method of dealing with moral questions. Our Saviour being as he was a loyal Israelite, can hardly be expected to have treated the law with levity, and in fact he said he was making it more binding. But the way in which he makes it more binding in the Sermon on the Mount is somewhat paradoxical; for it sometimes involves the setting aside of what appears to be commanded, and what is at least in fact a permission, such as that retributive justice should be exacted by the judges from the perpetrators of various offences. If you look at Christ's sermon, I think you will find that what he does is this. He takes the precepts of the ancient law just as they stand, he sets aside the elaborate system of casuistry by which the Doctors of Israel had made the law appear to apply to instances, and he says: 'Look at the law and consider what the Divine legislator who gave you as law – which after all, you must remember, was something enforceable by the courts – consider what one who gave you this as law had in his heart in the form of desire.' The disciple of Christ, therefore, sees the law as a lot of pointers to principles; he considers what the God who laid this down as penal law would desire us freely to do. He who forbade adultery, did he desire any sort of lustfulness unsanctified by marriage – and so on?

We observe in other parts of our Lord's moral teaching, that he was an innovator by comparison with the scribes of his time, in that he accepted the principle that precepts might conflict. It is no use saying that the duty to keep the Sabbath will never conflict with the duty to love your fellow; and in such cases we have got to do the thing that is more weighty, in the light of the two great commandments, that we should love God and our neighbour. Take the moral teaching of Christ as illustrated (say) in St Matthew's Gospel, add it all up and consider the method of our Lord's thinking, and you will see that he shows all respect for traditional and (in the Jewish view) divinely revealed principles, but that he does not in fact deduce the action of the good man simply from the rules. One is to judge the application of the rules by that which is good, that which God desires. Clearly in the mind of Christ there is no possible conflict between seeing with God's eyes and seeing what is intrinsically best. But the traditional rules lay down for you lines along which you can look, which will help you to see with God; and this will be seeing what is the best.

If I were trying to do morals not on the basis of the Christian revelation but as a purely rational enquiry, I should want to say that what is fundamental to the moral consciousness, or to the nature of duty, is just the pull exercised on a candid mind, on a decent man, by the personal being and need of his neighbour or of his own true nature; and that rules are all entirely subsidiary to this. It is absurd to say that if you pass by and see a child drowning in the canal you say to yourself, 'There is a rule that men who can swim should not allow children to drown in canals', or that you will then syllogise: 'I am a man who can swim, this is a canal, this is a child who is apparently drowning, and therefore the rule applies.' You have to pull the child out of the canal, because this is a child, and because it is intolerable the child should drown in the canal; and this has nothing to do with the existence of any moral rule, but is just the pull of the being of your fellow-creature; and this truth seems to me to be absolutely basic.

Our religion comes into this, if we are Christians, because we ask ourselves what it is in the other person which demands this measureless respect on our part. In the sort of case about which you can write an existentialist novel, one should be prepared to risk, or indeed to sacrifice, one's life for one's neighbour, as Christ indeed said, 'Greater love hath no man . . .' But for what in your neighbour must you sacrifice your life, or what in your neighbour demands your measureless respect? If your neighbour's physical existence is threatened, well it is a simple case; but most of our moral responses are not called upon by threats to our neighbours' existence. We think that it is good to make people happy, to let them have what they want; and yet surely it cannot be a duty to help people go to hell their own way, or be as wicked or foolish as they wish. It isn't my neighbour as a piece of meat who commands my moral responses, nor is it my neighbour as a person who entertains a certain number of actual wishes, many of which may be very bad; still less of myself can I think in that way, if I think I have duties to myself. But how shall I dare to say that what in my neighbour prescribes my duty and my action towards him is what I think he ought to be? How can any of us dare to advance such arrogance? Only a belief in God as the wise creator of us all, whose creative action is constantly proceeding, can give the Christian his way of thinking about that in his neighbour's existence which commands or should command his measureless response, or devotion.

The basis of morality is seeing with God, seeing with the God who makes all things and sees them to be good. We don't ask whether things are good because God makes them or whether he makes them because he sees that they will be good; we are sure that his work is good and if we can see with God, we are seeing what is also humanly good. If I can appreciate what is that core in my neighbour's heart which goes along with the divine creative work, or which is the work of God in him, then this coincides with what I see in him to be good and what demands my devotion.

Moral minds are minds that see with God; and of course no one can suppose that God in measuring what is good goes by rules. God is not a God of disorder and so no doubt there is an analogy, a rational analogy, between God's several actions and intentions. If there were not, woe to us, for how should we see our way about our world? But God does not presumably reason from moral rules, he sees that that which he wishes to create is good, or sees to it that it shall be good; and the analogy between the goodness of different things that he works at is as it were built into the things; and so of course to some extent with our own responses. If I disinterestedly love Peter and Paul, by loving them both, no doubt I am doing the same thing; but this does not involve any procedure from rules on my part, it just means yielding to the supremely rational impulse of appreciating what is there, or what God is doing there, and allowing the facts to move my mind into a rational response. So that I would say, if we are looking for the basis of morality, that it cannot be anything else than seeing with God; and since God does not proceed by rules, but from a direct vision, appreciation and intention of the things, morality cannot rest basically on rules.

Morality is not a divine dictation, with or without penalties and bribes, kicks and halfpence, attached; and in so far as high-minded atheists in deriding Christian morality as rejecting a system of parade-ground orders shouted at us by the Almighty with threats and promises attached to them, then anything that they may say about such a debased form of our religion is well deserved. But still there is much that we must say on the side of rules. God's thinking is not abstract, God does not presumably think in descriptive sentences containing universal terms; we do. We, in order to understand things, take them apart, into their universalisable aspects. God's mind must surely see things whole and entire without going through this absurd human process of taking things to pieces in order to put them together again; but we men are condemned to such absurdities, and this is just as true of our thought in the moral sphere as in any other sphere; so that our just seeing the child drowning in the canal and feeling the intolerableness of leaving him there, though a very speaking instance of the basis of moral feeling, is by no means typical of the whole of the business. If that were all, then there would not be systems of ethics nor would philosophers be discussing the matter. We don't simply react to compelling situations, we go through the humiliating game of understanding our moral world by verbal generalisations. So moral wisdom both can be and needs to be taught. If rules played no essential part in the matter we shouldn't teach children morality by giving them precepts. God doesn't have to talk to himself if he is to understand; we do.

But there is much more to be said about the necessity of moral rules. Not only do we need rules so that we may appreciate the finer points of value and of duty, by comparing one case with another, and so forth; we need rules so that we can form habits.[3] It is nonsense to say that we can get through our moral life by responding freshly and individually, and without any prejudice arising from previous thought or experience, to every new situation as it arises. Morality, as Aristotle wisely said, goes by habit and you cannot have a habit about anything but the operation of a rule. You cannot have a habit about how to treat unique situations uniquely. Moreover rules save us from much of this *Angst* which existentialist philosophers seem to take to be a merit. The existentialist goes through agonies in trying to add up the moral arithmetic of each particular situation. There are situations that call for such treatment, but they are comparatively few and if we had to go on like this all our lives we should all very soon be in the hands of psychiatrists. One has just got to be able to feel all right about telling the truth rather than lying on the whole, and so on, and so on, and so on; it will cause you too many agonies to work out the merits of the individual situation every time.

Further, rules are vital for co-operation and mutual trust, and this is very important; this is one of the chief difficulties of the existential position. We have not only got to know what we are doing ourselves, but we have got to be able to rely on what other people will do. This is one of the valid bases for a fairly fixed pattern of social mores; one simply cannot live with one's neighbours if we are all acting on the inspiration of the moment in assessing duty, and changing our philosophies day by day. And then there is the need for common witness – this is perhaps to anticipate, but the Christian at least has not only got to do what he thinks the Divine will lay upon him, he has got to do it so that it may be, to some extent, visible, and that he may be holding up the witness of a higher morality before the world; and unless we all co-operate in this, unless we all agree about the rules we are observing, nobody will possibly see what we are all up to, or what we are witnessing to.

I remember an anecdote I was told by a bright young person in the London government-sponsored radio. The anecdote was about his boss, the director, a Scotsman, of the old school.[4] Some of the young things were amusing him with charming tales of life in Bloomsbury and how A and B had exchanged wives without any formality and how nicely they were all four of them getting on together; at which the director broke out and said, 'But do ye condone it, man? Do ye condone it?' which they thought was awfully funny. Well in a way I can see it was funny, but in another way it does not seem to me to be all that funny. I mean, does one condone it? Is one going to say that there is no moral witness to be upheld? If there is a moral witness to be upheld, then those who are upholding it have got to keep certain rules, so that it can be seen that the corresponding principles are honoured.

And then to take a ground for the importance of rules which is perhaps more specifically Christian, I would say that situation ethics (the theory that you just assess each situation on its merits) is a Utopian system. It isn't merely that we cannot see the situation with the clarity of the divine mind and therefore need rules to help us, it just is that we cannot trust ourselves. This seems most clearly to be the case, as you must be very well aware, with sexual ethics. Supposing one says: 'No doubt self-control and fidelity and even chastity, if we still dare use the word, are good on the whole; but the situation may arise in which somebody has fallen in love with you so much that it is a terrible frustration to put them off.' It sounds reasonable, perhaps; but who do you think is to be trusted with the administration of that sort of elastic rule, considering what the sexual nature of all of us is like? What girl is not going to be taken in every time by the chalk-faced lover who says he is absolutely miserable and cannot possibly feel any better unless she will take him to bed? What girl is not going to fall for that, unless she has been given a principle, a rule that she is going to keep, to the effect that you just do not do it? Then there is something to hang on to. The pretence that we can solve problems like this by situational ethics is just a piece of pride; we are not like that. There are types of question, where we are not being judges so much in our own case, and not so much the victims of emotional delusion; but the same principle applies in some measure all over the field. Law is a remedy for original sin, for the bias of our nature, for the fact that we just won't judge straight when we think we are judging the matter on its merits; the rule gives us something to hang on to.

I hope it is clear that none of the things I have been saying about the obviously essential nature of moral rules does anything to undermine the principle that a moral action is not moral because a divine imperative has been shouted at us, or because there is some mystical value attaching to copybook precepts. One can see clearly enough that morality can consist in response to the demands of our personal environment and of our own integrity, our own nature, and that nevertheless, without the use of rules, morality is something that we cannot personally practise, nor co-operate with our neighbours in practising.

Now I have finished what was going to be the introductory part of this lecture, the question, so tempting to a philosopher, as to what is the essential nature of morality; but this is not what I was supposed to be talking about. However, now I am in a position to talk about what I was supposed to be talking about. Rules are vital to the existence of morality as a personal or social function, but that still does not mean that rules are unalterable. There must be rules or we cannot be moral, but it may well be that morality has laws and by-laws, laws that are unalterable and by-laws that are alterable from time to time. The traffic had better drive either on the right-hand side as in your country or on the left-hand side of the road as in my country, it is undesirable to mix these styles of driving, but it clearly does not matter which you adopt, so long as you stick to it. It is very immoral to drive on the right-hand side of the road in Great Britain or on the left-hand side of the road here, but this does not mean that either rule reposes on eternal necessity. I do nevertheless want to say, that to all evidence and quite apart from Christian revelation or anything of that kind, there are moral principles that have an eternal necessity. The debate that goes on between relativism and what we might describe as absolutism in morals, in so far as it is anything real and not just a scholastic exercise, is a debate about where the boundary between laws and by-laws should fall. We need not allow anybody to make our flesh creep by suggesting to us that when a lot of clever geneticists have bred man up into quite a different sort of animal, and a lot of clever mechanics have provided him with an infinite number of highly ingenious and adaptable gadgets, the moral rules that apply to our conduct here might none of them apply to the conduct of the imaginary and artificially developed man.

The principles in morality which are unalterable are those that express the essential nature of rational minds in mutual communication. Why shouldn't I tell lies? Because it is the frustration of the straight use of communication. Mentality as we possess it is a social phenomenon, we were talked into talking, and that means thought into thinking, by the parents and others who brought us up. Our minds only exist in mutual relation, and mutual communication; and lying is the frustration of communication. Therefore though there may be occasions when we have to do it, it's a pity. And so with all other principles that have the same sort of status. Whatever men may do to themselves or to the system by which they live interiorly or politically, it will never, by that charity and mutual regard, cease to have exactly the authority that they now have, if not an even greater authority. The same evidently with all the duties of fidelity and all those principles on which any intercourse between any community of minds whether human or angelic depends. These principles are unalterable because whatever happens to us we are going to remain incarnate social minds until we die. The by-laws on the other hand belong to the variable region.

The tendency of old-world thought was to put what we regard as by-laws in with the eternal laws. People say sometimes that the conception of natural law has vanished from the earth. This seems to me to be quite untrue for the reason I have given. There are principles of conduct which are bound up with the fact that we are minds or persons in mutual relation. The claims of natural law were, however, vastly inflated by ancient and medieval thought. Reaction has led people to say now that there is no such thing as natural law, i.e. anything unalterable or prescribed by our own nature itself.

The extreme on that side is represented by Marxist doctrine. Marx saw how greatly the social morals of different successive civilisations were influenced by the economic structure of those civilisations and above all, alas, by the interests of an exploiting class; and Marx is right. But Marxists have sometimes exaggerated the bearing of this so as to say that the Marxist who is living in bourgeois society, since he is not subject to the rules of that society, is freed from any moral controls, any obedience to rules of any kind, in dealing with the bourgeois world. So the Marxist is free to lie or to break his promises or anything like that in his dealings with capitalists, if he thinks that it will work. This as well as being a piece of political villainy is a theoretical error, resulting from a failure to see the difference between principles that are bound up with the very nature of personalities in relation, and principles that are the running principles of a certain sort of social set-up.

Our friend C. S. Lewis wrote a short but very fine piece of work (*The Abolition of Man*)[5] about the universality of basic moral principles. He demonstrated it on empirical lines by showing how surprisingly great was the agreement between primitive and civilised codes on the essentials. He also showed that what are considered to be striking variations in moral codes will frequently turn out not to affect basic principles at all but to derive from errors of factual opinion. The Aztecs were mild, amiable people, far less fierce than the Spaniards who destroyed them. On the other hand they sacrificed their fellow-beings by an extremely painful operation to the solar deity, because they held the erroneous view that if they did not do this, there was no guarantee that the sun would continue to revolve around the sky; and if the sun remained fixed either over the plain of Mexico or on the other side of the globe the results would be extremely awkward. So that these mild and amiable chaps, if we may regard them so, were doing their duty by the human race in the most amiable way they could by selecting victims, and tearing their hearts out of them with all the proper ritual, to keep the Sun-God going. They did not differ from us in thinking that one should be charitable and kind to one's neighbours, they just differed from us in an opinion about astronomy.

The burning questions that present themselves to us in our own time are really borderline questions, or borderline instances, or instances about which at least it is plausible to hold two opinions. Since it seems inevitable to talk about sexual morality in this connection, what do you say about it? On the one side it's plain that the pattern of sexual behaviour that has been admired, or regarded as according to the rules, has differed enormously in different tribal and cultural set-ups, and that our society is very different from society in the time of St Paul. It was very important in those days that a man should be sure that his children were his own and that the world should not be inundated with fatherless infants. We have found another way of dealing with that difficulty, a way that does not involve abstinence for anyone. St Paul held the view that while celibacy was excellent if you could stick it; if you could not stick it, you could always marry – it is better to marry than burn; so that anybody who is in the state of 'burning' in his phrase, should have marriage as a possible resource. Although no doubt there would be difficult cases, where people had got to be heroic for the sake of the Christian rule, yet unless the rule would work in general, the principles he lays down don't seem to apply. Now he supposes that the person who has reached that sort of physical maturity when the sexual urge is strongest will be in a position to marry; he also assumes, I think, that more or less any partner will do. That is to say, that if members of the Christian Church marry at this presumably early age when it is most difficult to control yourself, they will be able to make a go of it.

The case for rejecting the continued validity of St Paul's rules is well known. While we admit to being still the same animals and while we agree that some degree of control and the observance of some sort of pattern in sexual behaviour is required of us, as it was always required of mankind, we insist that our society is now quite different. We have learnt how to control conception and birth. Education has become too prolonged with all the things that we have to know, we give so much orange juice to children to bring them on physically, that the gap between puberty and an economically convenient age for marriage has become intolerable to the faithful disciples of St Paul. We can also say that we have become far more complicated beings and that it is no longer true for us that more or less any partner will do; that if people marry freely at the age when it seems physically most natural, they make unsatisfactory marriages which break up again. There is plenty you can say in argument for the thesis that the rules that seemed good to ancient Israel and indeed to Christ and his Apostles don't apply, as they stand, to our condition. What can you say on the other side?

St Paul devoted an epistle (1 Corinthians) very largely to sacramental questions. He insisted on the great spiritual importance of ceremonies connected with eating together – that if we eat together in a certain way this constitutes a spiritual bond, a tie-up that has eternal consequences. In the same letter he says that however much people think they can play about with sex, the divine intention is that sexual union, though as animal a thing as eating, should carry as heavy a spiritual charge; that if preserved for this use it becomes the basis of a unity that can make a cell in the body of Christ, and is a sacrament to us of our union with the divine; and to mix if I may St John with St Paul, he who cannot be faithful to the wife whom he has seen, how shall he be faithful to the Christ whom he has not seen? This is St Paul's positive teaching; his teaching is not based anywhere on the undesirability of the birth of fatherless children, or any of these things which so concern the secular moralist, but on the sacramental principle. So what do we say? St Paul's doctrine, which seems to me most profoundly and importantly philosophical, is based on a view about the incarnate nature of the human mind. I have been saying that there are manifestly unchangeable principles of morality connected with our rational nature; but it is also true that our biological nature as animals is as far as we know in principle unalterable. I do not know if any of the clever chaps who are playing about with genes are proposing to evolve a sexless race or if they do, how much thanks they will get from the advertising industry.

St Paul is alleging that there is a divinely intended tie-up between our rational nature as persons and these most lowly and physical functions, so that the nature of one should control the use of the other. I presume that this is what you and I are going to preach. But if so, we are going to be saying, are we not, that the society in which we live is desperately perverted not only in the way in which its individual members tend to go on or in the mores that they accept, but in its structure. If what St Paul says is true, then we ought to be living in such a way that people can marry at a natural age and under conditions that should make it reasonably hopeful that their unions would be stable. This is a very difficult thing to say yet must we not say it?

Now I come to a point which I ought to have covered far earlier. The great grievance of the sponsors of situational ethics against traditional Christian morality is that besotted as we are with our traditional rules, and with keeping them and being more holy than others, we close our minds to the solution of existing difficulties and the clearing up of existing situations. The problem here is certainly complex. Everyone, whether he be a Christian or not, who is at all a high-minded person, has the need presumably to live on two levels. He has got to accept, from the general run of men, current practice; has got to take them as they are, and deal with them, to some extent, according to their own lights. At the same time he himself feels the necessity to live by higher principles and to associate especially closely with people who share his own higher ideals and with whom he can share a life on that superior level.

This is a predicament that besets not only the Christian but every high-minded and serious group of people. Especially the Christian of course, because he has a supernatural mind to share with his fellow Christians. It is obvious that such a position whether taken by a Christian Church or by any other group brings forward two dangers, that of pharisaism and that of irrealism [*sic*]. Pharisaism, because you just draw away from people who don't keep your rules, when you say, 'This is the way to live; if you don't live by these rules or see fit to live by these rules, I have nothing to say to you', and this is in the extreme case, for example, the attitude of Christians who pretend that something called Christian opinion could impose upon a mixed or largely secular state a truly Christian set of laws about marriage and divorce. This is Pharisaism, but it is also irrealism because it means in fact contracting out of any attempt to deal with the actual difficulties of your fellow men. Obviously if we are asking whether the Christian accepts, or judges and rejects the contemporary world, it must be answered that we are not free to reject anything; and as for judging it, there is a divine precept on that subject. No doubt there are certain judgements that we do implicitly make by the way we live and by what we recommend. But clearly one has to start from where things are; to help other people solve their difficulties on principles which they can accept and by which they can live, while of course holding up the light of the Christian moral standard and trying to move things, even in the political field, as far in that direction as you really think they can be got to go.

Now it is plain that it is not only difficult to live on two levels at once, but it is an attempt in which we shall to a large extent fail; so that there is some truth in the humanist contention that the man who holds no principles and just professes situational ethics, who is prepared to look at any situation just as it is and try to make people happy, may often be more successful at judging objectively and making himself useful to mankind than the Christian, faithful to his Christian law, but perhaps not very able or large-minded. This seems to me to be just so. There is a great number of the Christian faithful who will never get beyond feeling that it is the thing to do what the rules and principles of their church call on them to do. They will do this because it is the will of God and out of fidelity to their Christian society; and all those who don't do it will be to them a lot of benighted scoundrels – one does not see what one can do for them except just keep on recalling the gospel to them. Such attitudes no doubt prevail far too widely. It's a nuisance that we shall diminish as far as we can, particularly in ourselves, by our pastoral handling of people who don't share all our convictions. But it is I would have said a nuisance well worth tolerating, as the negative shadow accompanying a positive witness. Surely we agree with Christ and St Paul that the Christian sacramental view of sex is something to be maintained at all costs. It must be upheld because it is true, and preserved for the sake of mankind, even through a period in which it will place the young Christian in situations of intolerable personal difficulty, and may even constitute a mild sort of martyrdom. After all, we were called to martyrdom and our chances of being martyred seem somewhat slim; and if we are to be martyred along these lines, it's a let-off.

To summarise: I have said that morality does not depend on rules but on valuations and appropriate responses, but that rules are essential instruments for the appreciation of value, for the regulation of response, and for mutual understanding. I have said further that such rules are either laws resulting from our very nature as persons in relation to one another, or by-laws differing with different structures of society; and that the burning issues about which people now talk are really matters that seem to lie between the two; for whatever theories people may profess about the basis of morality, nobody thinks that men are free to lie and cheat or that they ever will be so, and nobody thinks that by-laws are eternal necessities of our moral nature. So that these questions that people consider when they talk about a new morality simply concern the decision about where this boundary-line lies; and I have confessed that the Christian is likely to be inhibited in his judgement by a perfectionism that may lead him to be stiffly traditional; traditional, since one who is inclined to be holy in a corner will be inclined to go on being holy by the old rules, even when those rules may not altogether be valid. Yet his weakness is his strength, because he has through his fidelity to his faith a standard by which to judge existing societies and a treasure to preserve for the future blessing of mankind.

Notes

1 Before this paragraph, Farrer had typed but later crossed out the following two paragraphs:

Perhaps it might have made the best sense if I had switched the order of the last two lectures, because we have just about got to the place this afternoon, especially in question time, where one would want to go on and talk about what is valid and invalid in the criticism of the gospels. But without very much thinking, I am afraid, of how the series of topics would join on, I put down for the third lecture the most burning question of all – that about the adaptability of Christian moral rules.

The question as I phrased it was, 'Does Christian morality give way to a change in the social pattern, or is it the other way about?' Are we to adapt traditional moral rules so that they will fit, or apply to, a current social pattern or do we judge the pattern by its failure to come up to the rules?

2 Joseph Fletcher's *Situation Ethics* had been published in 1966 and John Robinson's *Honest to God* in 1963: talk of the 'new morality'

was much in the air and Farrer is here (partly) addressing this (see Fletcher, 1966; Robinson, 1963).

3 Farrer pre-empts the more recent rediscovery of Aristotle and virtue-based ethics in the wake of MacIntyre, 1981.

4 Almost certainly Farrer is referring to Lord Reith who was Director-General of the BBC and noted as someone keen on straight talking.

5 Lewis, 1944.

Epilogue

The Mark of Cain:
A Sermon for Evening Prayer

STEPHEN PLATTEN

Keble College, Oxford, 18 January 2019
Readings: Genesis 4.1–16, 25–26; Matthew 22.15–33

Most days of the week, for the past five years, I have travelled
to and from Bond Street to St Paul's on London's Central
Line, mornings and evenings, and using the escalators when
they're not being repaired! I remember one of Austin Farrer's
sermons reflecting on a similar experience. He quoted an
advert for women's undergarments, which ran: 'For Ladies,
for uplift, for general support.' Now, of course, such advertising would be well out of fashion – maybe even politically
incorrect.

Films and plays now feature most frequently on escalators and Underground station platforms. Prominent at present are *Stan and Ollie* and *The Favourite*. Some 60 years
ago, in Austin's time, equally prominent would have been
Elia Kazan's production of John Steinbeck's novel *East of
Eden*, starring the ill-fated idol of those days, James Dean.
Steinbeck's novel had been a roaring success with the punters,
and the film was equally fêted. The critics, however, panned
the novel arguing that Steinbeck's images were far too obvious. The symbolism he used sprang, of course, from our first
reading today. Steinbeck transferred that violence to two
Californian families.

Despite this controversy, the story of Cain remains one of the most memorably dark tales from the Patriarchs. Alongside Abraham and the sacrifice of Isaac, it is unforgettable. So, if we are to criticise the symbolism, then perhaps we need to lay that fault at the door of the *Jahwist*, or whoever contemporary critics believe to be the source of the original tale. It is effectively another description of the Fall, described elsewhere by the Priestly writer where it is set within Eden itself. Here tasting the fruit of 'the tree of good and evil' is the sharp image used for humanity's fallenness.

The tale of Cain is equally powerful: indeed, the Mark of Cain is a phrase that was absorbed into literature and wider culture, perhaps from as early as Patristic times onwards. It is a narrative riven with ambiguity – not only about humanity, but also about the nature of God. Let me remind you of the early verses:

And the Lord had regard for Abel and his offering, but for Cain and his offering he had no regard. So Cain was very angry, and his countenance fell.

The Almighty's response is equally sharp:

Why are you angry and why has your countenance fallen? If you do well, will you not be accepted? Sin is crouching at the door; its desire is for you, but you must master it.

There is much subtlety woven into the narrative – was Abel the divine favourite, or was this simply Cain's projection? If there truly was an imbalance from the start, then was this God's test of Cain's weak and contingent humanity? – and, if that was the case, then why was Abel the favourite of the Almighty – and if he was the favourite then that very fact would itself later bear mortally on his own destiny.

So, here we are treated to one of those determinative images that spring out of Holy Scripture in both Testaments. In some ways, the very violence of the story of Cain and Abel is an even more compelling and terrifying image than that of Adam and Eve, humanity's fabled proto-parents.

This terror springs from our ability to project, with our own perception, the universality of these great controlling images. Whether it be overweening jealousy within families, or innocent men stabbed on railway trains, or even the corruption of power within and between nations, the *Mark of Cain* has an eternal ring to it.

It is this, of course, developed in a remarkably subtle theological pattern, that remains perhaps Austin Farrer's most precious and lasting gift to Christian belief. In the most frequently quoted passage from *The Glass of Vision*, Farrer wrote:

> I would dare to think, that sometimes my thought would become *diaphanous*, so that there should be some perception of the divine cause shining through the created effect, as a deep pool, settling into clear tranquillity, permits us to see the spring in the bottom of it from which its waters rise.[1]

This, Farrer says, is how we encounter divine revelation. The resonances of these great images permeate our own thoughts and feelings – it is they that become diaphanous. So, this evening's first reading is one of the more vivid examples of one of those great images through which Scripture speaks. Cain's tale convicts us of powerful instincts within our own humanity and also of the ever-present possibility of divine response.

It is Jesus this time, in that second reading from Matthew's Gospel, who points to how the focus of our hearts does something similar – how our thought becomes diaphanous to the underlying truths. First, it is about what we would call social ethics in the question of tribute to Caesar; second, it is about marriage and individual relationships, as he remonstrates with the Sadducees on resurrection. Jesus, the very essence of the new covenant, points his hearers much more deeply to two underlying images – the transcendent authority of God and the power of the Resurrection.

We began with those countless flashes of publicity on London Underground escalators, which caught Farrer's eye – the very *earthiest* of starting points. Earthiness, albeit tragically transformed, is equally where the story of Cain began. It is where Steinbeck roots his book and his imagery, be it obvious or not; it is where Elia Kazan began animating those life-and-death images within a screenplay. So let me leave you with Holy Scripture, which was precisely where we began:

And the Lord put a *mark on Cain*, lest any who should come upon him should kill him. Then Cain went away from the presence of the Lord, and dwelt in the land of Nod, east of Eden.

Amen.

Note

1 Farrer, 1948, p. 8.

Bibliography of Works Cited

Altizer, Thomas J. J., 1966, *The Gospel of Christian Atheism*, Philadelphia, PA: Westminster Press.

Altizer, Thomas J. J. and William Hamilton, 1966, *Radical Theology and the Death of God*, Indianapolis, IN: Bobbs-Merrill.

Anonymous, 1968, Obituary: Rev A. M. Farrer, *The Times*, 30 December 1968.

Barfield, Owen, 1928, *Poetic Diction: A Study in Meaning*, London: Faber and Gwyer.

Barrett, C. K., 1956, Review of Austin M. Farrer, *Studies in St Matthew and St Mark*, *Journal of Theological Studies* 7: 107–10.

Bartsch, Hans Werner and Reginald H. Fuller, eds, 1961, *Kerygma and Myth: A Theological Debate*, New York: Harper & Row.

Brown, Warren S., Nancey C. Murphy, and H. Newton Malony, 1998, *Whatever Happened to the Soul? Scientific and Theological Portraits of Human Nature*, Theology and the Sciences, Minneapolis, MN: Fortress Press.

Bultmann, Rudolf, 1934, *Jesus and the Word*, trans. L. P. Smith and E. H. Lantero, New York: Scribner's.

Bultmann, Rudolf, 1958, *Jesus Christ and Mythology*, New York: Scribner's.

Cameron, Averil and Ian W. Archer, 2008, *Keble Past and Present*, London: Third Millennium.

Capon, Robert Farrar, 1965, *Bed and Board: Plain Talk About Marriage*, New York: Simon and Schuster.

Carey, John, 2014, *The Unexpected Professor: An Oxford Life in Books*, London: Faber and Faber.

Conti, Charles C., 1995, *Metaphysical Personalism: An Analysis of Austin Farrer's Metaphysics of Theism*, Oxford: Clarendon Press.

Cox, Harvey, 1965, *The Secular City: Secularization and Urbanization in Theological Perspective*, London: SCM Press.

Crombie, I. M., 2004, 'Austin Marsden Farrer (1904–1968) [rev. by Robert Brown]', *Oxford Dictionary of National Biography* 19: 121–3.

Cullmann, Oscar, 1958, *Immortality of the Soul or Resurrection of the Dead? The Witness of the New Testament*, London: Epworth Press.

Cupitt, Don, 1980, *Taking Leave of God*, London: SCM Press.

Cupitt, Don, 1997, *After God: The Future of Religion*, London: Weidenfeld and Nicolson.

Curtis, Philip, 1985, *A Hawk Among Sparrows: A Biography of Austin Farrer*, London: SPCK.

Davey, Francis Noel, 1952, Review of Austin Farrer, *A Study in St Mark, Journal of Theological Studies* 3: 239–42.

Drennan, Basil St George, ed., 1970, *The Keble College Centenary Register 1870–1970*, Oxford: Keble College.

Dunbabin, J. P. D., 1994, 'Finance since 1914', in *The History of the University of Oxford*, vol. 8 *The Twentieth Century*: 639–82, ed. B. Harrison, Oxford: Clarendon.

Farrer, Austin, 1943, *Finite and Infinite: A Philosophical Essay*, Westminster: Dacre Press.

Farrer, Austin, 1948, *The Glass of Vision*, Westminster: Dacre Press.

Farrer, Austin, 1949, *A Rebirth of Images: The Making of St. John's Apocalypse*, Westminster: Dacre Press.

Farrer, Austin, 1951, *A Study in St Mark*, Westminster: Dacre Press.

Farrer, Austin, 1952, *The Crown of the Year: Weekly Paragraphs for the Holy Sacrament*, Westminster: Dacre Press.

Farrer, Austin, 1954, *St Matthew and St Mark*, Westminster: Dacre Press.

Farrer, Austin, 1955, 'On Dispensing with Q', in *Studies in the Gospels: Essays in Memory of R. H. Lightfoot*, 55–88, ed. D. E. Nineham, Oxford: Blackwell.

Farrer, Austin, 1958, *The Freedom of the Will*, London: A&C Black.

Farrer, Austin, 1960a, *A Faith of Our Own*, Cleveland, OH: World Pub. Co.

Farrer, Austin, 1960b, *Said or Sung: An Arrangement of Homily and Verse*, London: Faith Press.

Farrer, Austin, 1961, 'An English Appreciation', in *Kerygma and Myth: A Theological Debate*, 212–23, ed. H. W. Bartsch and R. H. Fuller, New York: Harper & Row.

Farrer, Austin, 1962, *Love Almighty and Ills Unlimited: An Essay on Providence and Evil, Containing the Nathaniel Taylor Lectures for 1961*, London: Collins.

Farrer, Austin, 1963, 'Objections to Christianity', *Theology* 66: 317–18.

Farrer, Austin, 1964a, *The Revelation of St John the Divine: Commentary on the English Text*, Oxford: Clarendon Press.

Farrer, Austin, 1964b, *Saving Belief: A Discussion of Essentials*, London: Hodder and Stoughton.

Farrer, Austin, 1965, 'The Christian Apologist', in *Light on C. S. Lewis*, 23–43, ed. J. Gibb, London: G. Bles.

Farrer, Austin, 1967, *Faith and Speculation: An Essay in Philosophical Theology, Containing the Deems Lectures for 1964*, London: A&C Black.

Farrer, Austin, 1970, *A Celebration of Faith*, London: Hodder and Stoughton.

Farrer, Austin, 1973, *The End of Man*, London: SPCK.

Farrer, Austin, 1976a, *The Brink of Mystery*, ed. C. C. Conti, London: SPCK.

Farrer, Austin, 1976b, 'In His Image: In Commemoration of C. S. Lewis', in *The Brink of Mystery*, 45–7, ed. C. C. Conti, London: SPCK.

Farrer, Austin, 1976c, *Interpretation and Belief*, ed. C. C. Conti, London: SPCK.

Farrer, Austin, 1993, *Words for Life*, eds C. C. Conti and J. L. Houlden, London: SPCK.

Farrer, Austin M., 1966, *Love Almighty and Ills Unlimited*, The Fontana Library: Theology and Philosophy 409, London: Collins.

Fletcher, Joseph F., 1966, *Situation Ethics: The New Morality*, London: SCM Press.

Fuller, Reginald H., 1963, *The New Testament in Current Study: Some Trends in the Years 1941–1962*, London: SCM Press.

Gibb, Jocelyn, ed., 1965, *Light on C. S. Lewis*, London: G. Bles.

Goodacre, Mark, 1996, 'Goulder and the Gospels: An Examination of a New Paradigm', *Journal for the Study of the New Testament: Supplement Series* 133, Sheffield: Sheffield Academic Press.

Goodacre, Mark, 2001, *The Synoptic Problem: A Way through the Maze*, London: Sheffield Academic.

Goodacre, Mark, 2002, *The Case against Q: Studies in Markan Priority and the Synoptic Problem*, Harrisburg, PA: Trinity Press International.

Goodacre, Mark, 2008a, 'Mark, Elijah, the Baptist and Matthew: The Success of the First Intertextual Reading of Mark', in *Biblical Interpretation in Early Christian Gospels*, Vol 2: *The Gospel of Matthew*: 73–84, ed. T. R. Hatina, Library of New Testament Studies 310, London/New York: T & T Clark.

Goodacre, Mark, 2008b, 'Redaction Criticism', in *Searching for Meaning: An Introduction to Interpreting the New Testament*, 38–44, ed. P. Gooder, London: SPCK.

Goulder, Michael D., 1977–1978, 'On Putting Q to the Test', *New Testament Studies* 24: 218–34.

Goulder, Michael D., 1985, 'Farrer the Biblical Scholar', in *A Hawk Among Sparrows: A Biography of Austin Farrer*, ed. P. Curtis, London: SPCK.

Goulder, Michael D., 1989, 'Luke: A New Paradigm', *Journal for the Study of the New Testament: Supplement Series* 20, Sheffield: Sheffield Academic Press.

Goulder, Michael D., 1996, 'Is Q a Juggernaut?', *Journal of Biblical Literature* 115: 667–81.

Goulder, Michael D., 1999, 'Self-Contradiction in the IQP', *Journal of Biblical Literature* 118: 506–17.

Green, Roger Lancelyn and Walter Hooper, 1974, *C. S. Lewis: A Biography*, London: Collins.

Halsey, A. H., 1994, 'The Franks Commission', in *The History of the University of Oxford*, vol. 8 *The Twentieth Century*: 721–36, ed. B. Harrison, Oxford: Clarendon.

Hebblethwaite, Brian, 2007, 'The Philosophical Theology of Austin Farrer', *Studies in Philosophical Theology* 40: x–123.

Hedley, Douglas and Brian Hebblethwaite, eds, 2006, *The Human Person in God's World: Studies to Commemorate the Austin Farrer Centenary*, London: SCM Press.

Henson, Shaun C., 2016, 'Is Someone Killing the Great Academic Priests of the Western World?', in *Academic Vocation in the Church and Academy Today*, 9–30, ed. S. C. Henson and M. J. Lakey. Farnham: Ashgate.

Hick, John, 1957, *Faith and Knowledge: A Modern Introduction to the Problem of Religious Knowledge*, Ithaca, NY: Cornell University Press.

Hick, John, 1970, 'Freedom and the Irenaean Theodicy Again', *Journal of Theological Studies* 21: 419–22.

Hick, John, ed., 1977, *The Myth of God Incarnate*, London: SCM Press.

Hollis, Adrian, 2001, 'Spencer Barrett', *The Guardian*, 16 October 2001.

Hooper, Walter, 1996, *C. S. Lewis: A Complete Guide to His Life and Works*, San Francisco, CA: HarperSanFrancisco.

Kennedy, Darren, 2011, *Providence and Personalism: Karl Barth in Conversation with Austin Farrer, John Macmurray, and Vincent Brümmer*, Oxford/New York: Peter Lang.

Kloppenborg, John S., 2003, 'On Dispensing with Q? Goodacre on the Relation of Luke to Matthew', *New Testament Studies* 49: 210–36.

Kloppenborg, John S., 2014, 'Is There a New Paradigm?', in *Synoptic Problems: Collected Essays*, 39–61, Wissenschaftliche Untersuchungen zum Neuen Testament 329, Tübingen: Mohr Siebeck.

Lakoff, George and Mark Johnson, 1980, *Metaphors We Live By*, Chicago/London: University of Chicago Press.

Levering, Matthew, 2019, *Did Jesus Rise from the Dead? Historical and Theological Reflections*, Oxford/New York: Oxford University Press.

Lewis, C. S., 1939, 'Bluspels and Flalansferes: A Semantic Nightmare', in *Rehabilitations and Other Essays*, 135–58, London: Oxford University Press.

Lewis, C. S., 1942, *A Preface to Paradise Lost*, Ballard-Matthews Lectures 1941, Oxford/London: Oxford University Press.

Lewis, C. S., 1944, *The Abolition of Man: Or, Reflections on Education with Special Reference to the Teaching of English in the Upper Forms of Schools*, London: Humphrey Milford/Oxford University Press.

Lewis, C. S., 1947, *Miracles: A Preliminary Study*: 220pp, London: G. Bles/The Centenary Press.

Lewis, C. S., 1958, *Reflections on the Psalms*, London: G. Bles.

Lewis, C. S., 1967, 'The Language of Religion', in *Christian Reflections*, 159–74, ed. W. Hooper, Grand Rapids, MI: Eerdmans.

Lewis, C. S., 1969, *Selected Literary Essays*, ed. W. Hooper, Cambridge: Cambridge University Press.

Lewis, C. S., 1979, *God in the Dock: Essays on Theology*, ed. W. Hooper, London: Fontana.

Lewis, C. S., 2000–2006, *Collected Letters*, ed. W. Hooper, 3 vols, London: HarperCollins.

Lloyd, Michael, 1996, 'The Cosmic Fall and the Free Will Defence', D.Phil. dissertation, University of Oxford.

Lloyd, Michael, 1998, 'Are Animals Fallen?', in *Animals on the Agenda*, 147–60, ed. A. Linzey and D. Yamamoto, London: SCM Press.

Lloyd, Michael, 2018a, 'The Fallenness of Nature: Three Nonhuman Suspects', in *Finding Ourselves after Darwin: Conversations on the Image of God, Original Sin, and the Problem of Evil*, 262–79, ed. S. P. Rosenberg, Grand Rapids, MI: Baker Academic.

Lloyd, Michael, 2018b, 'Theodicy, Fall, and Adam', in *Finding Ourselves after Darwin: Conversations on the Image of God, Original Sin, and the Problem of Evil*, 244–61, ed. S. P. Rosenberg, Grand Rapids, MI: Baker Academic.

Loades, Ann and Robert MacSwain, eds, 2006, *The Truth-Seeking Heart: Austin Farrer and his Writings*, Norwich: Canterbury Press.

Lummis, E. W., 1925–6, 'The Case Against Q', *Hibbert Journal* 24: 755–65.

MacIntyre, Alasdair C., 1981, *After Virtue: A Study in Moral Theory*, Notre Dame, IN: University of Notre Dame Press.

MacSwain, Robert, 2008, 'A Fertile Friendship: C. S. Lewis and Austin Farrer', *The Chronicle of the Oxford CS Lewis Society* 5.2: 22–44.

MacSwain, Robert, 2013, *Scripture, Metaphysics, and Poetry: Austin Farrer's The Glass of Vision, with Critical Commentary*, Ashgate Studies in Theology, Imagination, and the Arts, Farnham: Ashgate.

Mascall, E. L., 1978, 'Austin Marsden Farrer (1904–1968)', *Proceedings of the British Academy* 64: 435–42.

McLeish, Alexander, 1934, 'The World Dominion Movement: Its Ideals and Activities', *International Review of Mission* 23: 215–24.

Milbank, John, 1990, *Theology and Social Theory: Beyond Secular Reason*, Oxford: Blackwell.

Mitchell, Basil, 1957, 'Introduction', in *Faith and Logic: Oxford Essays in Philosophical Theology*, 1–8, ed. B. Mitchell, London: Allen & Unwin.

Mitchell, Basil, 2005, 'Staking a Claim for Metaphysics', in *Faith and Philosophical Analysis: The Impact of Analytical Philosophy on the Philosophy of Religion*, 21–32, ed. H. A. Harris and C. J. Insole, Heythrop Studies in Contemporary Philosophy, Religion and Theology, Aldershot: Ashgate.

Moltmann, Jürgen, 1985, *God in Creation: An Ecological Doctrine of Creation. The Gifford Lectures 1984–1985*, London: SCM Press.

Neill, Stephen and N. T. Wright, 1988, *The Interpretation of the New Testament: 1861–1986*, Oxford/New York: Oxford University Press.

Nielsen, Jesper Tang and Mogens Müller, eds, 2016, *Luke's Literary Creativity*, Library of New Testament Studies, London: Bloomsbury/T&T Clark.

Nineham, Dennis, 1994, 'Foreword: Michael Goulder – An Appreciation', in *Crossing the Boundaries: Essays in Biblical Interpretation in Honour of Michael D. Goulder*, xi–xv, ed. S. E. Porter et al., Biblical Interpretation 8, Leiden: Brill.

Peterson, Jeffrey, 2000, 'A Pioneer Narrative Critic and his Synoptic Hypothesis: Austin Farrer and Gospel Interpretation', *Society of Biblical Literature Seminar Papers* 39: 651–72.

Poirier, John C. and Jeffrey Peterson, eds, 2015, *Marcan Priority Without Q: Explorations in the Farrer Hypothesis*, Library of New Testament Studies, London: Bloomsbury/T&T Clark.

Polkinghorne, J. C., 2003, *Living with Hope: A Scientist Looks at Advent, Christmas and Epiphany*, London: SPCK.

Richardson, Alan and John Bowden, eds, 1983, *A New Dictionary of Christian Theology*, London: SCM Press.

Robinson, John A. T., 1963, *Honest to God*, London: SCM Press.

Ropes, James Hardy, 1934, 1960, *The Synoptic Gospels*, 2nd impression with new preface, Cambridge, MA/London: Harvard University Press/Oxford University Press.

Sanders, E. P., 1993, *The Historical Figure of Jesus*, London: Allen Lane/Penguin.

Slocum, Robert Boak, 2007, *Light in a Burning-Glass: A Systematic, Presentation of Austin Farrer's Theology*, Columbia, SC: University of South Carolina Press.

Southgate, Christopher, 2008, *The Groaning of Creation: God, Evolution, and the Problem of Evil*, Louisville, KY: Westminster John Knox Press.

Streeter, B. H., 1924, *The Four Gospels: A Study of Origins, Treating of the Manuscript Tradition, Sources, Authorship, & Dates*, London: Macmillan.

Teilhard de Chardin, Pierre, 1959, *The Phenomenon of Man*, London: Collins.

Thomas, Keith, 1994, 'College Life, 1945–1970', in *The History of the University of Oxford*, vol. 8 *The Twentieth Century*: 189–216, ed. B. Harrison, Oxford: Clarendon.

Titley, Robert, 2010, *A Poetic Discontent: Austin Farrer and the Gospel of Mark*, Library of New Testament Studies 419, London: T&T Clark.

Van Buren, Paul M., 1963, *The Secular Meaning of the Gospel, Based on an Analysis of its Language*, Library of Philosophy and Theology, London: SCM Press.

Vidler, Alec R., 1963a, 'Historical Objections', in *Objections to Christian Belief*, 57–78, ed. D. M. MacKinnon et al., London: Constable.

Vidler, Alec R., 1963b, 'Introduction', in *Objections to Christian Belief*, 7–10, ed. D. M. MacKinnon et al., London: Constable.

Ward, Keith, 1969, 'Freedom and the Irenaean Theodicy', *Journal of Theological Studies* 20: 249–54.

Ward, Keith, 1970, *Ethics and Christianity* (repr. Routledge 2002), London/New York: Allen & Unwin/Humanities Press.

Ward, Michael, 2005, 'The Son and the Other Stars: Christology and Cosmology in the Imagination of C. S. Lewis', PhD dissertation, University of St Andrews.

Weaver, Richard M., 1984, *Ideas Have Consequences*, Chicago/London: University of Chicago Press.

Wiles, Maurice F., 1974, *The Remaking of Christian Doctrine*, Hulsean Lectures 1973, London: SCM Press.

Williams, Rowan, 2001, *Arius: Heresy and Tradition*, 2nd edn, London: SCM Press.

Williams, Rowan, 2018, *Christ the Heart of Creation*, London: Bloomsbury Continuum.

Wilson, S. A. et al., 1986, *Anglicans and Racism: The Balsall Heath Consultation 1986*, Race Pluralism and Community Group, London: Board for Social Responsibility of the Church of England.

Wolfe, Judith, 2010, 'C. S. Lewis on Power', in *The Cambridge Companion to C. S. Lewis*, 174–88, ed. R. MacSwain and M. Ward, Cambridge: Cambridge University Press.

Wolterstorff, Nicholas, 1987, *Lament for a Son*, Grand Rapids, MI: Eerdmans.

Wright, N. T., 1999, *New Heavens, New Earth: The Biblical Picture of Christian Hope*, Grove Biblical Series 11, Cambridge: Grove.

Wright, N. T., 2003, *The Resurrection of the Son of God*, Christian Origins and the Question of God 3, London: SPCK.

Wroe, Martin, ed., 1992, *God: What the Critics Say*, London: Hodder and Stoughton.

Index of Scripture References

Index of Names and Subjects